YOUR
SEED WITHIN

YOUR SEED WITHIN

Harnessing Life Force for Energy, Confidence & Clarity

DARRIN ELFORD

Your Seed Within: Harnessing Life Force for Energy, Confidence & Clarity

Copyright © 2025 by Darrin Elford

First published by Darrin Elford 2025

The information contained within this book is strictly for information and educational purposes only. If you wish to apply the ideas contained in this book, you are taking full responsibility for your actions.

ISBN: 978-1-991363-35-0 (Paperback)

eISBN: 978-1-991363-36-7 (E-Book)

First edition

Acknowledgements

I want to express my heartfelt gratitude to my family and friends for their unwavering support throughout this journey. To my mentors and teachers, thank you for your wisdom and guidance, which have been instrumental in shaping the ideas within this book.

A special thank you to my editor and publishing team for your dedication and expertise in bringing this project to life. Finally, to you, the reader, thank you for choosing to embark on this journey of growth and self-discovery. May you harness the energy within you and unlock your full potential.

Table of Contents

Introduction

Why This Book?

Let's be real.

If you're holding this book, chances are something deep inside you is tired. Tired of feeling drained. Tired of wasting your energy. Tired of living small. You know there's more to life—but somehow, you've been stuck in the same loop. Click, release, regret. Over and over. I wrote this book because I've lived that loop.

There was a time when I was addicted to porn, low on energy, lost in my own head, and full of shame. I didn't respect myself. I looked in the mirror and didn't like the man staring back. I tried to fake confidence, distract myself with work, with women, with entertainment—but deep down, I felt empty.

The turning point came when I stopped looking *out there* for answers… and started looking *within*.

That's when I discovered semen retention—not just as a "hack" or a temporary challenge, but as a life-changing practice. A return to my natural power. My clarity came back. My energy exploded. I stood taller. My goals felt real again. And most importantly, I started to respect myself. Not because of what I achieved, but because of who I was becoming.

This book is for the man who wants that too. It's for the guy who's done with living at half-power. For the man who's ready to reclaim his confidence, his focus, his masculinity—and maybe even his soul. I won't sugarcoat things. The journey isn't easy. But it's worth it. Every step you take moved you forward.

This book is your roadmap from depletion to power, from confusion to clarity, from the coomer to the king. Whether you're just starting out or you've tried and failed a hundred times, this book is here to walk with you, every step of the way. Not to judge you. Not to preach at you.

But to remind you: **You are more powerful than you've been led to believe.**

The War on Your Vital Energy

From the moment you wake up, there's a battle going on—one that most people don't even realize they're fighting. It's not on a battlefield, and there are no flashing warning signs. But it's real. It's quiet. And it's constant.

It's the war on your vital energy.

Your vital energy is the life force that powers your body, your thoughts, and your spirit. It's what gives you clarity when the world feels chaotic. It fuels your confidence when doubt tries to creep in. It's the spark that makes you *you*—bold, alive, and full of purpose.

But here's the truth: the modern world is draining it. It happens in small ways. The constant buzzing of notifications. The pressure to keep up. The endless scrolling that numbs your mind. The food that fills your stomach but starves your soul. The noise. The rush. The never-ending demand to be "on," even when you're exhausted. You weren't designed to live like this.

Over time, this quiet war chips away at your energy. You feel tired even after a full night's sleep. You start questioning yourself. Your spark dims, your confidence fades, and your clarity turns to fog. You're running on empty, and you don't know why. But here's the good news: the war might be real, but so is your power. In this book, we're going to reclaim it.

We'll reconnect with your seed within you—the source of energy, confidence, and clarity that's been there all along. We'll uncover simple, powerful ways to protect your energy, recharge your spirit, and return to the version of yourself you may have forgotten but never lost.

Because when you stop giving your energy away to everything and everyone else, something amazing happens: You come back to life.

A Personal Note: From Rock Bottom to Radiance

I didn't write this book from a mountaintop—I wrote it from the floor.

There was a time in my life when everything felt heavy. My energy was gone. Confidence? Non-existent. Clarity? I was just trying to make it through the day without falling apart. On the outside, I might've looked like I had it together. But inside, I felt like I was running on empty. It was more than burnout—it was like my inner light had dimmed, and I didn't know how to turn it back on.

One night, after another day of pretending I was okay, I found myself sitting in the dark—physically and emotionally. I had nothing left to give. That's when I whispered a quiet prayer, not even sure who was listening: *"There has to be more than this."*

That whisper turned into a search. A search for what I now call the **seed within**—a hidden spark of life force that exists in all of us. It's not something you get from outside sources. It's something you remember. Something you *awaken*. And once you do, it changes everything.

This book is the journey of how I found that spark, how I nurtured it, and how it grew into strength, confidence, and deep clarity. I want you to know that no matter where you are—whether you're just tired, totally lost, or somewhere in between—your radiance is still there. Your power didn't disappear. It just got buried.

I'm not here to fix you. You're not broken. I'm here to remind you that everything you need is already inside you. You are the seed. And you have more life force than you've ever been told. Let's begin.

How to Use This Book

Your Seed Within is meant to be more than just something you read—it's a guide you come back to again and again. Whether you're looking for more energy, inner confidence, or clarity in your life, this book offers tools to help you connect with your life force—your inner power, the "seed" within.

You don't have to read it all at once. You can start at the beginning and move through it chapter by chapter, or you can jump to the parts that speak to you most right now. Each chapter stands on its own and offers simple practices, reflections, and ideas you can use right away.

Here are a few tips to help you get the most out of it:

- **Take your time.** There's no rush. Let each idea sink in and give yourself space to feel and explore.

- **Try the practices.** Many chapters include short exercises to help you apply what you're learning. You don't have to do them all—just the ones that feel right for you.

- **Use a journal.** Writing down your thoughts and experiences can help you connect more deeply with your inner self and track your growth.

- **Come back often.** As you grow, you might notice new insights or meanings in things you've already read. Let this book grow with you.

This is your journey. Let the words guide you, but always listen to your own truth first. The power is already within you—you're just learning how to unlock it.

1

The Fall – Life as a Coomer

The Digital Abyss: Porn, Dopamine and Disconnection

Let's be real—this world we're living in is full of distractions. And one of the biggest ones, the one most people are too ashamed to talk about, is porn. Porn promises quick pleasure, instant relief, and zero consequences. But what it really delivers is emptiness.

Behind the screen, it feels like you're getting something. A hit of dopamine here, a rush of desire there. But the truth is, every click is silently pulling you further away from yourself. Further from your power, your presence, and your purpose.

Here's what's happening: your brain is wired to reward you for things that help you survive—food, connection, sex. When you watch porn, your brain floods with dopamine, the "feel-good" chemical. But because there's no real connection, no real intimacy, it becomes a loop—watch, release, regret. And then, repeat. Over time, this rewires your brain. Real life starts to feel dull. Real relationships feel like work. Real intimacy? Too scary. Too slow.

So instead, we turn to the screen again. And again. And again. But here's the cost: your energy drops. Your confidence fades. Your clarity disappears. You start feeling numb, anxious, even angry—and you don't know why. You lose touch with your spark. Your masculinity feels hollow. Your mind becomes foggy. And most importantly, you become disconnected from the seed within—your life force.

This isn't just about porn. It's about what happens when we chase artificial highs instead of real, grounded connection with life. With our bodies. With others. With ourselves.

And here's the truth no one tells you: **you're not broken.** You're just stuck in a system designed to keep you addicted and distracted. But you can wake up. You can break free.

This chapter is your wake-up call. We're not here to shame the past. We're here to reclaim your power.

Symptoms of Energy Depletion

When your life force is low, everything feels harder. You might not notice it at first. It creeps in slowly—like a phone battery draining in the background while apps are still running. But over time, the symptoms become harder to ignore.

Here are some common signs that your energy is being drained:

1. Constant Tiredness (Even After Sleep)

You wake up feeling just as exhausted as when you went to bed. No matter how much you rest, you never feel fully recharged.

2. Mental Fog

It's hard to focus. Your mind feels cloudy. You forget things, zone out during conversations, or struggle to make decisions.

3. Low Motivation

Even simple tasks feel overwhelming. You keep putting things off—not because you're lazy, but because your energy tank is empty.

4. Mood Swings & Irritability

Small things get under your skin. You feel anxious one moment, down the next. It's like your emotions are always on edge.

5. Disconnection

You feel distant—from others, from your body, from your purpose. Things that used to excite you don't hit the same anymore. Life feels flat.

6. Addictive Patterns

You find yourself reaching for quick fixes—porn, scrolling, sugar, caffeine, weed, whatever gives a temporary "hit." But it never lasts, and you always end up back where you started—or worse.

7. Lack of Confidence

You doubt yourself more. You second-guess your words, your actions, your worth. You feel like a shell of who you know you *could* be.

These are all signs that your life force—your inner energy—is being leaked, blocked, or suppressed. The good news? This is not permanent. Energy can be restored. Confidence can return. Clarity can rise again. But first, you need to get honest. Recognize what's been draining you. That's where healing begins.

The Cycle of Shame, Addiction and Regret

Let's talk about the loop—the one so many people are stuck in but hardly anyone speaks about out loud. It starts with a craving. Maybe it's stress. Boredom. Loneliness. A moment where you just want to escape. So you reach for something easy—something that gives you a quick hit: porn, junk food, scrolling, substances, whatever your mind thinks will help you "feel better."

For a few minutes, it works. You feel good. You forget. But then, the crash comes. You don't feel better—you feel worse. You regret it. You beat yourself up. You wonder, *Why did I do that again?* You feel weak. Disconnected. Ashamed.

That shame sinks deep, and instead of healing it, you try to hide it. You pretend everything's fine. But inside, it's not. That shame grows, and the more it grows, the more you want to escape it. So the craving comes back. And the cycle starts all over again.

Craving → Acting Out → Temporary Relief → Regret → Shame → Craving Again.

This is the trap. This is how addiction works—not just to substances or porn, but to patterns of escape. And it's not just about what you're doing—it's about what you're *trying not to feel.*

Here's the truth:

You're not broken. You're not weak. You're not alone.

You're stuck in a pattern your nervous system learned to survive. But what once helped you cope is now holding you back. And you're here because some deeper part of you knows it's time to break free. Freedom doesn't come from more willpower or more self-hate. It comes from awareness. From compassion. From learning how to meet yourself differently.

We break the cycle not by fighting ourselves—but by understanding ourselves. By facing the shame, not running from it. By feeling what we've been avoiding. And by learning how to reconnect with the deeper source of strength that's been inside us all along. That's what this book is about.

The Lie of Instant Gratification

We live in a world that runs on speed. Everything is one click away—food, pleasure, entertainment, validation. Don't feel good? Swipe, tap, scroll, consume. You'll feel better in seconds... right? That's the lie of instant gratification.

It *feels* like relief. It *looks* like pleasure. But underneath, it's empty. Fleeting. Hollow. A sugar rush for the soul that leaves you crashing harder every time.

You know the feeling:

The moment you hit play on a video you shouldn't be watching. The late-night binge.

The 30 minutes you spent scrolling and now can't even remember what you saw. That quick "yes" to comfort that turns into a long "why did I do that?". Instant gratification is a trap because it gives you the illusion of control while actually taking it away. It feeds your urges but drains your energy. It gives you comfort but steals your confidence. It silences your discomfort but never solves it. And the worst part? It convinces you that you can't handle real life without it. But here's the truth:

Real fulfilment takes time.

Real growth takes effort.

Real power comes from patience, not shortcuts.

Every time you resist the pull of instant gratification, you reclaim a piece of your power. You tell your brain, *I don't need a quick fix—I'm building something real.* That's how you restore your energy. That's how you rebuild your confidence. That's how you reconnect with the seed within.

So the next time you feel the urge to chase a cheap high, pause. Breathe. Ask yourself: *Is this helping me feel more alive—or just numbing me from what I don't want to feel?*

Freedom doesn't come from more—It comes from choosing *better*.

Why You Feel So Empty

You've probably asked yourself this before:

Why do I feel like something's missing, even when everything looks fine?

Why do I feel so hollow inside, like I'm just going through the motions?

This feeling of emptiness—it's not weakness. It's not failure. It's a signal. A message from deep inside you that something important has been ignored for too long.

Here's the truth:

You weren't made to live disconnected, distracted, and drained. But modern life encourages exactly that. It pulls you away from your body, your heart, your purpose. You trade your time for screens, your energy for comfort, your attention for noise. You reach for quick highs and lose the ability to sit with stillness. And in all of that rushing and numbing...You lose touch with your inner world. You forget what you truly need. You forget *who you really are*. That emptiness you feel? It's not a void to fear. It's a space that's waiting to be filled— with presence, with purpose, with truth.

But here's the catch: real fulfilment doesn't come from the outside. Not from pórn. Not from likes. Not from money, status, or someone else's approval. It comes from within. From reconnecting with your life force—your seed. From turning inward instead of always running outward. From finally meeting the parts of you that you've been avoiding, suppressing, or silencing.

You feel empty because you've been living outside of yourself. You feel empty because you've been trying to fill a spiritual hunger with physical distractions. You feel empty because you've been taught to chase everything *except* your true self. But the good news is: emptiness is not the end. It's the beginning. It's the space where transformation can happen—if you're willing to stop running and start listening. This book is your map. But the journey? That's yours.

2

The Hidden Power of Your Seed

Semen as Life Force: More Than Just Fluid

Let's strip away the shame and get honest. Semen isn't just some waste product your body needs to get rid of. It's not just a "release." It's not just about sex or pleasure. Semen is life force. It's power. It's concentrated creative energy.

Think about it: in just one drop of semen are millions of cells capable of creating *life*. That's not a small thing. That's sacred. That's potent. That's raw, untapped energy your body worked hard to produce.

In ancient cultures—from Taoism to yogic traditions—semen was seen as a vital essence. Not something to throw away, but something to *honor*. Something to *contain, refine,* and *channel.* And yet, today, we live in a world that treats it like it's nothing. Endless porn. Endless "release." Endless draining.

The truth is, every time you ejaculate, you're not just losing fluid—you're giving away energy. Physical energy. Mental energy. Spiritual energy. You might feel good for a moment, but afterward? You feel tired. Dull. Disconnected. Your drive fades. Your clarity blurs. Your edge softens.

That's not a coincidence. Your seed carries the blueprint of life. When you protect it, you feel stronger, sharper and more grounded. When you waste it, you feel weaker. Foggy. Unstable.

This isn't about fear or control. It's about *awareness*. It's about realizing that you carry something sacred inside you—something powerful. And when you learn to hold it, direct it, and honor it… something changes. You start walking differently. Thinking differently. Living differently. You begin to embody what so many men have lost: **presence, clarity, confidence, and purpose.** So no, your semen is not "just fluid." It's your seed. And how you treat it says everything about how you treat yourself.

Eastern Perspective: Tantra, Taoism & Brahmacharya

In the East, there's a deep reverence for the body's life force. Ancient traditions didn't just see energy as something to be used up or discarded—they saw it as something sacred, something to be preserved, cultivated, and directed.

This is where practices like Tantra, Taoism, and Brahmacharya come in—each offering a profound way of understanding and harnessing our life force, especially our sexual energy.

Tantra: Harnessing Sacred Energy

In Tantra, sexuality isn't just a physical act—it's a spiritual practice. The idea is that sexual energy is one of the most powerful forces in the human body, and when used consciously, it can be a pathway to deep spiritual growth and enlightenment.

Rather than seeing orgasm as a release to be quickly sought, Tantra teaches us to *slow down* and focus on *connection*. It's about feeling every sensation, understanding the energy that's rising within you, and using it to expand your awareness. Through this, you can transmute the energy of the body into something higher—leading to greater spiritual awakening and deep intimacy with yourself and your partner.

When practiced mindfully, Tantra allows you to access and amplify your life force rather than drain it. The energy you once released carelessly becomes fuel for your body and soul.

Taoism: The Alchemy of Sexual Energy

Taoism, one of the oldest philosophical and spiritual traditions, has a similar approach. According to Taoist teachings, sexual energy, or *jing*, is one of the most precious resources a person has. In Taoism, the idea is to conserve and transform this energy, using it to enhance life, longevity, and vitality.

Taoist practices like *semen retention* (often referred to as *nei kung*) teach that when a man refrains from releasing semen, he can retain his life force. By holding onto this energy, he nourishes his body, strengthens his vitality, and cultivates greater clarity and peace. Instead of expelling energy, the Taoist practitioner learns how to circulate it through the body, directing it upwards to nourish the mind and spirit.

Taoist philosophy also emphasizes *balance*. Life is about harmony between the yin (feminine) and yang (masculine). By mastering sexual energy, you gain the ability to control the flow of your life force, helping to align your inner energies with the natural rhythms of the universe.

Brahmacharya: The Path of Self-Mastery

Brahmacharya, a key concept in Hinduism and yoga, often translates as "celibacy," but it's more than just abstaining from sex. It's about self-control, self-discipline, and the wise management of your energy. Brahmacharya teaches us to channel our sexual and creative energy toward higher purposes—whether through spiritual practices, creative endeavors, or physical vitality.

The practice of Brahmacharya is rooted in the belief that when sexual energy is not wasted or overindulged, it can be transformed into a potent source of strength and clarity. It's about cultivating *conscious* choices—whether in relationships, sexuality, or how we spend our time. By conserving this energy, a person can elevate their consciousness, improve their mental state, and deepen their connection with the divine.

In all three traditions—Tantra, Taoism, and Brahmacharya—the core principle is the same: **Sexual energy is sacred.** When respected and harnessed, it becomes one of the most powerful forces for transformation, clarity, and growth.

This ancient wisdom can feel like a distant world in today's fast-paced, distraction-filled society. But by bringing some of these teachings into your life, you can begin to reclaim your energy, restore your vitality, and step into a new way of living—one that honors the power of your life force.

Would you like to explore how to begin integrating some of these practices into your daily life, or go deeper into the physical benefits of conserving your life force?

Insights: Testosterone, Neurochemistry & Retention

While the ancient traditions of Tantra, Taoism, and Brahmacharya offer profound insights into the power of sexual energy, modern science has also started to uncover the physiological and psychological benefits of conserving that energy. Specifically, the relationship between semen retention, testosterone, and neurochemistry has been the subject of growing interest.

Testosterone: The Hormonal Powerhouse

Testosterone is more than just the "male hormone." It plays a critical role in everything from muscle mass and strength to mood, energy, and overall vitality. It influences your confidence, your drive, and even your sense of well-being. It's no surprise that many people, especially men, are searching for ways to boost it.

What happens when you conserve your sexual energy—through practices like semen retention—is that your body naturally produces more testosterone. In fact, studies have shown that testosterone levels can peak after just a few days of abstinence from ejaculation. This spike may explain why many people report feeling more energetic, more focused, and even more confident when they practice retention.

One study conducted by Michael Exton and his colleagues in 2003 showed that testosterone levels increased significantly after three days of abstinence from ejaculation, and that level remained elevated for up to a week. This suggests that periodic abstinence from ejaculation could be a natural way to optimize testosterone production and, by extension, physical and mental performance.

Neurochemistry: Dopamine, Serotonin, and the Brain's Reward System

When we engage in behaviors that give us pleasure—such as eating, socializing, or even sex—our brain releases a powerful chemical called dopamine. Dopamine is the brain's reward chemical, the one that makes us feel good, motivated, and ready to take action.

But there's a catch: Overstimulating your brain with constant "quick hits" of pleasure—whether from excessive pornography, social media, or instant gratification—can cause the brain to become desensitized to dopamine. The result? You need more and more stimulation to get the same effect, and you start feeling less and less satisfied with the things that used to bring you joy.

This is where retention comes into play. By practicing conscious abstinence and allowing your dopamine system to reset, you can recalibrate your brain's reward system. Instead of constantly chasing the next "high," you begin to appreciate the simple, everyday pleasures of life—creating a natural state of well-being and satisfaction.

Interestingly, when you practice retention, your brain also increases the production of serotonin, another neurochemical linked to mood regulation and feelings of happiness. Higher serotonin levels can make you feel more stable, calm, and centered—an antidote to the anxiety and restlessness many people feel when they're stuck in the cycle of instant gratification.

The Power of Retention: Mental Clarity and Cognitive Function

Beyond the hormonal and chemical changes, many people who practice semen retention report feeling clearer mentally. They feel more focused, more driven, and more creative. This isn't just coincidence—it's a result of the way your body's energy is being used.

When you conserve sexual energy, your body doesn't just redirect that energy to physical processes. It also supports cognitive function. The brain requires energy to process information, think critically, and make decisions. By retaining your seed, you stop the depletion of energy that might otherwise be used in repeated ejaculation, and your body has more resources to fuel the mind.

In a sense, you become more "sharpened." People who practice retention often experience heightened alertness, better concentration, and improved memory. They feel less mentally foggy and more in control of their thoughts and emotions.

The Bottom Line

Both science and ancient wisdom agree on this: energy is valuable. Whether it's testosterone boosting your vitality or dopamine resetting your brain's reward system, semen retention taps into the body's natural chemistry to enhance your mental and physical health.

Instead of treating your sexual energy as something to be spent and drained, you can choose to retain it, harness it, and channel it into a life of greater focus, vitality, and clarity. By respecting your body's rhythms, you don't just preserve energy—you transform it.

Your Seed is You: A New Way to See Yourself

What if you could see yourself not just as a collection of thoughts, body parts, or fleeting emotions—but as a vessel of limitless potential? What if you realized that the energy you carry inside you is the same energy that could shape your reality?

Your seed, your life force, is more than just a biological substance—it's the essence of who you are. It holds the power to create, to build, to sustain, and to transform. When you learn to see your seed as sacred and powerful, you begin to see yourself differently. You stop viewing your energy as something to be wasted, but something to be honored, cultivated, and protected.

A Sacred Gift

In traditional teachings, semen is often referred to as the *seed of life*. It carries the potential for creation—not just on a physical level, but on a deeper, more spiritual one. Your seed is a symbol of your creative power. It is the essence of your vitality, your masculinity, your strength. And when you release it too freely, you are not just giving up a physical substance—you are giving away your creative potential.

By shifting your perspective, you start to recognize that every drop of seed is an offering. What you choose to do with it reflects what you choose to do with your life force. Are you letting your energy drain into fleeting pleasures, or are you channeling it into something meaningful—your purpose, your creativity, your relationships, your growth?

A Reflection of Self-Worth

How you treat your seed is a direct reflection of how you value yourself. If you view your energy as expendable—something to be drained for temporary pleasure or distraction—you send a message to your subconscious that your worth is tied to external satisfaction, not inner strength. You begin to feel disconnected, depleted, and ungrounded.

On the other hand, when you begin to conserve and honor your energy, you make a statement to the universe about your self-respect. You are telling yourself that you have something valuable to give, and you are worthy of channeling that energy into something far greater than momentary relief. You start to reclaim your sense of purpose and strength. Your seed becomes a reflection of your true self—your potential, your vitality, and your power.

The Creative Power Within

Consider this: In one single moment, your seed contains all the genetic material required to create life. What would happen if you started to see that same creative energy as the fuel for *all* of your creations—not just biological, but personal, professional, and spiritual?

This is the invitation: to see your seed not just as a biological function but as your life's most potent creative force. Whether you're building a career, nurturing a relationship, or pursuing a passion, this energy can become the driving force behind everything you do.

When you channel that energy with purpose and intention, you unlock an infinite well of creativity, focus, and strength. You become the architect of your own life—creating not just in the physical sense, but in every aspect of your existence. Your seed is a symbol of infinite possibility.

Reclaim Your Energy, Reclaim Yourself

By respecting your seed and preserving your energy, you reconnect with the truth of who you are: not just a body, but a force of nature. You are a creator, a builder, a being of immense power. Every time you make the choice to conserve your seed, you make a deeper commitment to yourself and your highest potential. You stop being at the mercy of fleeting desires and start mastering your energy, your mind, and your life.

So, ask yourself: How do you want to see yourself?

Do you want to be someone who's constantly chasing empty pleasures and feeling drained? Or do you want to be someone who recognizes the sacred power within them and uses it to create a life that truly reflects their worth and potential?

Your seed is you. And when you treat it with respect and reverence, you begin to see yourself in a whole new light—as a being of immense power, creativity, and potential.

Dispelling Myths About "Blue Balls" & Health Risks

You've probably heard of the term "blue balls" before. It's a common phrase that gets thrown around when someone is left sexually frustrated—often in the context of feeling physical discomfort after sexual arousal without release. But let's take a moment to unpack this and dispel the myths surrounding it, especially in relation to your health and energy.

What Are "Blue Balls"?

"Blue balls" is a colloquial term for a temporary feeling of discomfort or mild pain that some men experience in the testicles after prolonged sexual arousal without orgasm or ejaculation. The sensation arises from increased blood flow to the genital area during arousal, but no release of that built-up energy. The blood vessels in the area become engorged, and while it's not typically harmful, it can be uncomfortable.

However, it's important to note that this is a *temporary* condition, and it's not dangerous. It's not a medical emergency. It can feel like a pressure or mild ache, but it generally resolves itself within a short time—either through ejaculation or simply waiting for the body to return to a balanced state.

The Myth: Blue Balls are a Sign of a Health Crisis

One of the biggest myths surrounding "blue balls" is that it's a serious medical condition or a risk to your overall health. In reality, the discomfort from blue balls is not harmful. While it might feel uncomfortable, it's not a threat to your physical well-being. No permanent damage occurs if you experience blue balls, and it certainly won't impact your fertility or reproductive health.

What's more, there's no medical evidence suggesting that not ejaculating or engaging in semen retention poses any long-term health risks. Your body is designed to handle periods of sexual arousal without ejaculation. In fact, many men practice semen retention for spiritual, psychological, and physical benefits without experiencing negative consequences.

The Real Health Risks: Overindulgence & Habitual Ejaculation

While blue balls themselves aren't a serious health risk, there are real health concerns associated with excessive or habitual ejaculation. Frequent release, particularly through behaviors like excessive porn consumption or habitual masturbation, can lead to the depletion of your energy, as we've discussed in previous sections.

Over time, regularly expelling your seed without purpose or mindful intent can drain your vitality, cause mental fog, reduce testosterone levels, and negatively impact your emotional well-being. You might feel depleted, anxious, or disconnected—none of which are symptoms of true health.

Additionally, there are psychological risks to constantly seeking sexual release for the sake of instant gratification. This habit can foster a cycle of addiction, where you're using sexual release as a way to cope with emotional discomfort or stress. Over time, this can erode self-control, diminish your sense of confidence, and leave you feeling trapped in unhealthy patterns.

The Truth About Semen Retention

One of the main concerns people have when they consider semen retention is the fear of physical discomfort, like blue balls, or the belief that it's unnatural. The truth is, *semen retention is a natural and healthy practice* for those who choose it, especially when approached with awareness and balance.

When practiced consciously and with intention, semen retention allows you to redirect that energy into more productive, creative, and fulfilling pursuits. The initial discomfort or temptation to release may arise, but it fades as your body adjusts and your energy is redirected into other areas of your life.

If you're practicing semen retention and you do experience temporary discomfort, there's no need to panic. Simply redirect your energy through physical activity, deep breathing, or focusing on creative endeavors. Over time, your body will become accustomed to retaining its life force, and the discomfort will diminish.

Conclusion: Listen to Your Body

It's important to listen to your body, not to myths or exaggerated claims. If you experience discomfort from sexual arousal without release, it's usually a temporary, harmless situation that will pass. And if you're considering semen retention as a practice, know that your body is more resilient than you may think. The discomfort of "blue balls" doesn't have to be a barrier, and it's not a sign that you're doing harm to yourself.

Remember: Your seed is precious. Treating it with respect and using it mindfully can unlock a level of vitality, mental clarity, and creative power that goes far beyond the fleeting moments of pleasure. In fact, by practicing retention consciously, you may find that you have even more energy and focus—both in and out of the bedroom.

3

The Awakening

Hitting Rock Bottom (and Why It's a Gift)

It's the moment we all dread, yet, at some point, we've all been there: when life feels like it's crumbling, when everything you've built seems to be slipping through your fingers, and you're left standing in the rubble, wondering how you got here. Maybe it's a failed relationship, a career setback, or the overwhelming weight of shame and guilt that keeps pulling you down.

But here's the thing about hitting rock bottom: *it's not the end.* In fact, it's often the beginning of something far greater than you can imagine right now.

You see, when you reach your lowest point, when you feel like there's nowhere else to go, something powerful happens. You stop running. You stop hiding. You stop pretending that everything is okay. For the first time, you're forced to face yourself—your fears, your weaknesses, and the parts of you that you've been avoiding for so long. In that raw, painful honesty, *you find your strength.*

The Gift of Clarity

Rock bottom doesn't feel like a gift at the moment. It feels like defeat. But in the stillness of that place, you can hear what's really been going on beneath the surface. You can hear the whispers of your soul, the ones you've ignored in your pursuit of pleasure, comfort, or validation.

When everything falls apart, you're left with only the truth. The distractions fade. The noise quiets. And in that space, you begin to see clearly—not just what's broken, but what needs to be rebuilt. You begin to understand what *really* matters, what *you* truly need, and what has been standing in the way of your growth.

Rock bottom brings clarity. It reveals the things you've been afraid to confront—the habits, the lies, the fears that have been keeping you stuck. And when you see those things for what they are, you have the power to change them. You can choose to rise from this place, to rebuild your life on a foundation of truth, authenticity, and purpose.

The End of One Chapter, the Beginning of Another

In the darkness of rock bottom, it might feel like you've hit a dead end. But the reality is that you've simply reached the end of a chapter. This chapter—the one where you were stuck in unhealthy patterns, numbing your pain, seeking instant gratification, or living in denial—has come to its close. Now, you're standing at the threshold of something new.

Rock bottom clears the slate. It gives you the chance to break free from the cycle that has been draining your energy, your confidence, and your sense of self. It forces you to ask the tough questions: *Who am I really? What do I really want? What kind of life do I want to create?*

When you allow yourself to honestly answer those questions, you're not just surviving—you're beginning to awaken. You're beginning to understand that you don't have to stay in this place. You can rise, stronger and wiser than before.

The Gift of Transformation

It's easy to see rock bottom as a punishment, but in reality, it's a call to transform. It's the universe (or life itself) pulling you out of your old way of being and offering you a chance to evolve.

This moment of breakdown can be the catalyst for your breakthrough. It's the moment you decide that enough is enough—that you're ready to step into a new version of yourself. A version that's not afraid to face discomfort, not afraid to face the truth, and not afraid to walk away from the things that have been holding you back.

This is the awakening. The moment when you realize that your greatest strength lies in your ability to rise from the ashes. That your true power comes from your ability to face the hardest moments of your life and still choose to move forward, choose to grow, and choose to evolve.

Moving Forward with Purpose

So, if you're in that place right now—feeling lost, broken, or stuck—know this: *Rock bottom is not the end.* It is a gift. It is an opportunity for transformation. It is the moment when you strip away everything that isn't truly you and begin to rebuild your life from a place of truth, power, and clarity.

You don't need to have it all figured out right now. The path forward may not be clear, but the fact that you're still standing, still breathing, still willing to face yourself—is a testament to your strength.

The real gift of rock bottom is not the pain. It's the awakening that follows. It's the realization that you are more resilient, more capable, and more powerful than you've ever known. And it's from this place that you begin to create a life that is aligned with your true purpose and your highest potential. So, take a deep breath. Embrace this moment. Because it's not just your lowest point—it's the beginning of your greatest rise.

What Happens When You Stop Releasing

The idea of stopping or reducing the frequency of ejaculation can be met with skepticism or curiosity. After all, we live in a culture where sexual release is often seen as a necessary outlet for stress, a mark of vitality, or even a symbol of masculinity. So, what happens when you choose to stop releasing, whether temporarily or long-term? What are the physical, mental, and emotional shifts that occur when you begin practicing semen retention?

Let's explore how your body, mind, and spirit respond when you stop releasing.

1. Increased Energy and Vitality

One of the most immediate effects of semen retention is a noticeable increase in energy levels. This is because when you release semen, your body expends a significant amount of energy—both physical and chemical. Semen is rich in nutrients, hormones, and minerals, and expelling it requires your body to work hard to replace what's lost.

When you retain your semen, your body no longer needs to allocate resources to replenishing this loss. Instead, your vital energy is conserved and redirected into other areas of your life. Many men who practice semen retention report feeling more energetic, less fatigued, and more motivated to take on challenges. You may also notice that your physical performance, whether in the gym or in everyday activities, improves.

But it's not just about physical energy. When your body is no longer drained by frequent ejaculation, your mental energy is also restored. You'll likely feel more focused, clear-headed, and driven. This increase in mental clarity comes from the simple fact that your body is no longer in a constant state of recovery from sexual release—it can now direct its resources towards more productive mental processes.

2. Higher Testosterone Levels

Testosterone is the hormone that governs much of your physical and mental strength—your drive, motivation, libido, and even your mood. There is evidence to suggest that abstaining from ejaculation can lead to an increase in testosterone levels.

For instance, a study conducted by Michael Exton in 2003 showed a peak in testosterone after three days of abstinence. While the increase was temporary, it highlights the potential for retention practices to have a positive effect on hormonal balance. Over time, consistent retention can help maintain more stable and elevated testosterone levels, leading to improvements in physical strength, confidence, and assertiveness.

Higher testosterone also contributes to improved mood. Men often report feeling more grounded, centered, and capable of taking on life's challenges when practicing semen retention. It's not just about physical changes; it's about emotional strength too.

3. Improved Mental and Emotional Clarity

When you stop releasing, you may begin to notice a shift in your emotional state. For many, frequent ejaculation—especially when coupled with the habitual consumption of pornography—can contribute to feelings of guilt, shame, or emotional numbness. These emotional states can cloud your judgment and rob you of your clarity.

By retaining your semen, you stop reinforcing these negative cycles. Your mind becomes clearer, and you're no longer weighed down by the emotional fallout that often accompanies frequent sexual release. You may find yourself less anxious, less dependent on external validation, and more in tune with your true emotions.

This clarity extends to your decision-making and your ability to stay focused on your long-term goals. When your energy is no longer being drained, you'll find yourself thinking more clearly, making more deliberate choices, and engaging with life from a place of intention, rather than reaction.

4. Heightened Creativity and Focus

Many practitioners of semen retention report a surge in creativity and productivity. This is because the energy that would otherwise be expended in sexual release is now being channelled into your creative and intellectual pursuits. Whether you're an artist, entrepreneur, or simply someone looking to improve at your work or hobbies, this extra energy can be harnessed to fuel your passions.

Retention also leads to better focus. Without the distractions of habitual sexual activity or the mental fog that comes with constant releases, your attention span becomes sharper. Tasks that once felt draining or difficult to complete may suddenly feel more manageable and rewarding. Whether you're writing a book, working on a business project, or even learning something new, you'll likely find that your mind stays more engaged, more present, and more productive.

5. Deeper Connection with Your Inner Power

At a deeper, spiritual level, semen retention can help you reconnect with your inner power. By consciously choosing not to release, you cultivate self-discipline, willpower, and the ability to make choices based on higher purposes rather than instant gratification.

This sense of control over your sexual energy can foster a deeper connection with yourself. You begin to realize that you are not defined by your urges or desires but by your ability to control them. You move away from feeling like a passive participant in your desires and become an active creator of your own life.

Over time, this sense of mastery over your energy can help you align with your higher self, fostering a stronger sense of purpose and a deeper connection to your spiritual practices. You may find that your meditation, prayer, or other spiritual practices become more profound as you tap into the life force you're preserving.

6. Improved Relationships and Increased Charisma

Another fascinating effect of semen retention is the positive impact it can have on your relationships and how you interact with others. When you retain your seed, you carry an energy that is magnetic and charismatic. This is not just physical energy—it's an energy that speaks to your confidence, your sense of self-control, and your emotional grounding.

As you stop expending your energy unnecessarily, you find that your relationships—whether romantic, familial, or platonic—become more fulfilling. You are less likely to seek validation or approval from others, and instead, you engage from a place of self-assurance and emotional stability. This can lead to deeper, more authentic connections with others.

Conclusion: A Shift in Power

So, what happens when you stop releasing? The answer is simple: *You reclaim your power.* You reclaim your energy, your clarity, your creativity, your drive, and your emotional stability. By conserving and redirecting your sexual energy, you unlock new l evels of vitality, strength, and purpose. It's not about abstinence for the sake of deprivation, but about conscious choice, self-mastery, and living in alignment with your highest potential.

When you choose to stop releasing, you choose to start living fully—from a place of purpose, power, and infinite possibility.

Internal Resistance: Shame, Urges & Withdrawal

Choosing to practice semen retention can be one of the most empowering decisions you make, but it's not without its challenges. As you begin this journey, you will inevitably face internal resistance—shame, urges, and even withdrawal symptoms that can feel overwhelming at times. These are natural responses, and understanding them is the first step toward overcoming them.

It's important to remember that internal resistance is part of the process, not a sign that you're doing something wrong. In fact, the very fact that you're facing resistance shows that you are making a powerful shift, breaking free from old habits, and stepping into a new phase of growth. Let's take a closer look at the common forms of internal resistance you might encounter and how to navigate them.

1. Shame: Breaking Free from the Conditioning

One of the first hurdles many men face in the process of semen retention is the feeling of shame. In a culture that often links masculinity and vitality to sexual release and constant gratification, abstaining from ejaculation can feel like you're doing something "unnatural" or "wrong." These societal beliefs can create a deep sense of shame around your sexual energy, making it difficult to embrace the practice of retention.

Shame often arises when you start to question deeply ingrained behaviors and beliefs. It's the voice that tells you, *"This isn't normal,"* or *"You're depriving yourself."* But the truth is that semen retention has been practiced for centuries in various spiritual and philosophical traditions, such as Taoism, Tantra, and Yoga. These traditions view sexual energy as sacred, and they recognize that when channelled properly, it can lead to profound personal growth, creativity, and vitality.

To overcome the shame, it's important to challenge the societal narratives around sexuality. Understand that your sexual energy is not something that should be used or discarded without intention. It's a powerful life force that, when treated with respect, can enhance your overall well-being. Release the shame by affirming that you are reclaiming your energy for a higher purpose—not depriving yourself, but strengthening yourself for greater accomplishments.

2. Urges: The Pull of Instant Gratification

Perhaps the most immediate and powerful form of resistance is the surge of sexual urges. When you choose to abstain from ejaculation, your body will naturally experience a buildup of sexual energy. These urges can feel intense, especially in the beginning, and they may challenge your commitment to retention. It's the body's way of reminding you that it's used to a certain pattern of behavior—and now it's asking for release.

These urges are completely natural, and they don't mean you're failing. They simply reflect your body's habit of seeking immediate gratification. It's important to recognize that urges, no matter how intense, do not have to control you. They are temporary sensations, like waves in the ocean. They come and go.

The key to navigating these urges is to not fight them, but to redirect them. Instead of succumbing to the impulse to release, use techniques to transmute that energy into something more constructive. Physical exercise, deep breathing, creative pursuits, or focusing on a personal goal can help channel the energy into something productive. The more you practice redirecting the energy, the easier it will become to remain in control.

3. Withdrawal: The Emotional and Psychological Detox

Just as someone might experience withdrawal symptoms when breaking a physical addiction, you may encounter emotional and psychological withdrawal when you start practicing semen retention. This is especially true if you've spent years relying on sexual release as a coping mechanism for stress, anxiety, or emotional discomfort.

Initially, you may feel more irritable, anxious, or restless. These feelings can be difficult to manage, but they're a sign that you're detoxing from the habitual need for instant gratification. You are breaking free from the cycle of using sex or ejaculation as a form of emotional release. As with any detox process, the initial discomfort is temporary, and on the other side is a stronger, more resilient version of yourself.

During this phase of withdrawal, be kind and patient with yourself. Instead of judging the discomfort, treat it as an opportunity for growth. It's a chance to explore the emotions, memories, or habits that may have been fueling your dependency on sexual release. Embrace the discomfort as part of the process and use it as motivation to stay committed to your practice.

4. The Power of Persistence

As you continue with your practice, the internal resistance will begin to lessen. The urges will become less frequent and less intense. The shame will start to dissipate as you gain more confidence in your ability to retain your energy and channel it into more meaningful pursuits. And the withdrawal symptoms will fade as you adapt to a new, healthier way of managing your emotions and desires.

Persistence is key. You are reprogramming your mind and body, and like any form of growth, it takes time. But every moment you resist the urge to release and redirect your energy into something more productive is a victory.

Remember: *Your greatest strength lies in your ability to overcome resistance.* By facing the discomfort head-on and choosing to stay true to your commitment, you are building the willpower, self-control, and discipline that will serve you in all aspects of life.

5. Turning Resistance into Power

Ultimately, overcoming internal resistance is a process of transforming your raw urges and emotional turbulence into something greater—your creative power, your mental clarity, and your emotional strength. Instead of letting shame, urges, and withdrawal dictate your behavior, you begin to see them as opportunities to grow stronger, more centered, and more self-aware.

Every time you face an urge, a wave of discomfort, or a moment of doubt, you are building resilience. You are training your mind and body to not rely on external sources for gratification, but to cultivate an inner reservoir of strength and power. With time, this transformation will extend beyond your practice of retention—it will influence every area of your life, from your work to your relationships to your personal growth.

Defining Your Why: The Fire that Fuels Retention

The journey of semen retention is not just a physical practice; it's a mental, emotional, and spiritual one. It requires patience, discipline, and, most importantly, a deep sense of purpose. Without a clear understanding of *why* you're doing it, the temptation to fall back into old habits can become overwhelming.

This is where defining your *why* becomes crucial. Your "why" is the internal fire that fuels your practice, the reason that propels you forward even when the challenges arise. It's the reminder of why you chose this path in the first place, and it's what will keep you grounded when you face urges, resistance, or moments of doubt.

But what is your *why*? How do you define it in a way that's meaningful to you? Let's explore how to tap into the power of your personal reason for retaining your energy and how it can transform your experience.

1. The Power of Purpose

Purpose is what gives life direction. It's the sense of meaning that drives you out of bed each morning, pushes you to be your best, and sustains you through tough times. Without purpose, life can feel like a series of random events, and your actions may feel disconnected from any deeper vision.

When you choose to practice semen retention, you're making a conscious decision to go against the current of instant gratification, to reclaim your life force, and to channel it into something greater. But to sustain this choice, you must connect with a deeper sense of purpose—a reason that transcends the physical act of retention.

Your *why* might be personal, and that's okay. Perhaps you're seeking increased vitality and energy to achieve your goals. Maybe you want to elevate your creative potential and improve your focus. Perhaps it's about mental clarity, emotional stability, or strengthening your relationships. Whatever it is, your *why* will be the compass that keeps you aligned with your path, helping you move forward with unwavering determination.

2. Clarity of Vision: Where Do You Want to Go?

To define your *why*, you must first be clear about where you want to go. Semen retention is not about merely abstaining from sexual release; it's about redirecting your energy towards creating the life you desire. Ask yourself: *What do I want to achieve?*

Do you want to:

- Build a more powerful, focused mind to excel at work or personal projects?

- Feel more emotionally grounded and confident in your relationships?

- Unlock your creative potential and tap into new levels of inspiration?

- Cultivate spiritual growth, find deeper self-awareness, and feel more connected to your purpose in life?

Whatever your vision may be, your *why* will guide you toward it. The more clearly you define your goals, the easier it will be to stay committed to your practice of retention. This clarity will act as your anchor when you face temptation or moments of discomfort, because you'll always know what you're working toward and why it matters.

3. Aligning with Your Highest Self

Semen retention isn't just about abstaining from sexual release—it's a form of self-mastery. It's about aligning with your highest self, the person you are meant to become, rather than the version of yourself that is driven by immediate desires or fleeting pleasures.

Your *why* is often tied to this idea of self-actualization—the desire to become the best, most authentic version of yourself. You might be seeking to break free from old patterns, unhealthy attachments, or the cycle of seeking external validation. The decision to retain your energy is, at its core, a decision to honor your fullest potential and not settle for less.

Ask yourself: *What does the best version of me look like?*

Perhaps you see yourself as someone who is:

- Disciplined and focused, not easily distracted by temptation or mindless habits.

- Calm and centered, able to stay grounded in challenging situations.

- Creative, inspired, and full of ideas that serve a greater purpose.

- Physically strong, healthy, and capable of achieving your fitness goals.

- Emotionally intelligent, with deep, meaningful connections to others.

Your *why* should be tied to this vision of your highest self. When you focus on becoming the person you were meant to be, retaining your energy is no longer about deprivation—it's about empowering yourself to live at your fullest potential.

4. Using Your Energy for Greater Impact

Another powerful aspect of defining your *why* is the recognition that your energy can be used for far more than fleeting pleasure or temporary distractions. Semen is often called "life force" because it carries immense potential. When you stop releasing without purpose, you free up this powerful energy to channel into meaningful pursuits—whether that's personal growth, creative work, building relationships, or contributing to the world in a way that leaves a lasting impact.

Think about the positive changes you want to make in your life and the world around you. Your *why* might be rooted in a desire to contribute something greater than yourself—a project, a cause, or a relationship that requires your full energy and attention. When you retain your seed, you are conserving and refining your energy to use it for your highest aspirations.

Ask yourself: *What do I want to contribute to the world?*

When you focus on the greater impact your energy can have—whether that's creating art, building a business, or simply being a better person for those around you—you begin to see your practice of retention as a tool for greater good. You're not just holding back for the sake of holding back; you're preserving your life force to make a real difference.

5. Staying Committed: The Fire That Fuels You

Your *why* is the fire that keeps you going, especially during the moments when the path feels challenging. There will be times when you feel tempted to revert to old habits, or when the discomfort of retaining seems unbearable. It's during these times that your *why* will be the most crucial.

Revisit your reasons regularly. Remind yourself why you started this journey in the first place. The clearer and stronger your *why*, the more powerful your ability to stay committed. You're not simply practicing retention for its own sake— you're doing it to build a better, more empowered version of yourself, and that vision will help you push through resistance.

Conclusion: Fuelling Your Journey

Your *why* is the spark that ignites your practice of semen retention. It's what turns a difficult process into an empowering journey. By defining your purpose— whether it's to boost your energy, focus your mind, align with your highest self, or contribute to something greater—you are giving yourself the strength to stay committed, even when the road gets tough.

Remember, this journey is yours. Your *why* is unique to you, and it will evolve as you grow. But the key is to connect with that deeper sense of purpose, and let it guide you through the ups and downs of your retention practice.

With a clear *why*, every challenge becomes an opportunity to strengthen your resolve, and every step forward brings you closer to the life you're meant to create.

Writing the First Page of Your Comeback Story

Every great story begins with a moment of choice—the decision to turn the page and start something new. If you're reading this, then you've already made that choice. You've decided that it's time for change, that it's time to step into a new chapter of your life. But as with any great story, the first page can feel intimidating. The blank canvas, the unknown path ahead, and the fear of failure may make it hard to believe that your comeback is even possible.

But let me tell you this: *Your comeback is already in motion.*

Right now, as you read these words, you are standing at the beginning of a new chapter. The beauty of this moment lies in the realization that *you get to write it.* You are the author of your own life, and the first page of your comeback story is waiting for you to fill it with courage, determination, and a vision for what comes next.

1. Recognize the Power of Starting Fresh

A comeback doesn't happen overnight—it's a journey. The first page of your story might seem small in the grand scheme of things, but don't underestimate its power. It's the beginning of a transformation. Right now, you are leaving behind the old version of yourself—the habits, beliefs, and cycles that held you back—and stepping into a new identity. This is where your story of growth, resilience, and self-mastery begins.

It's important to recognize that starting fresh doesn't mean erasing your past; it means taking the lessons you've learned from it and using them to fuel your future. You are not defined by your mistakes or setbacks. In fact, they are part of what will make your comeback so powerful. They are the challenges you've overcome, the obstacles that have shaped you, and the lessons you'll carry with you as you move forward.

So, take a deep breath and embrace the feeling of starting over. This is your opportunity to rewrite your narrative and set the stage for the success, fulfilment, and growth you deserve.

2. Define Your Vision for the Future

The first page of your comeback story isn't just about where you've been—it's about where you're going. You need a clear vision for the future. What does your ideal life look like? Who do you want to become? What are your goals, and what kind of person will you need to be to achieve them?

Take a moment to reflect on these questions. Envision yourself living the life you desire. See yourself full of energy, confidence, and purpose. What does that version of you look like? How does it feel to be in that place? The clearer your vision, the stronger your motivation will be to push through any obstacles that arise along the way.

Your comeback is about transformation, and transformation starts with a vision of who you want to become. Define your *why*—the purpose behind your comeback—and let that vision serve as your guiding light, always pointing you toward the future you're creating.

3. Embrace the Courage to Begin

Writing the first page of your comeback story requires courage. The past may have been filled with mistakes, regrets, or missed opportunities, but none of that matters now. The only thing that matters is that you've chosen to move forward.

Embrace the courage it takes to take that first step, even when you don't have all the answers or the road ahead is uncertain. Remember, every successful journey begins with uncertainty and discomfort. But each small action you take in the direction of your comeback is a victory. You don't need to have it all figured out—you just need to begin.

The key is to trust the process. Each day, commit to taking at least one small action that moves you closer to the person you want to be. Whether it's practicing self-discipline, redirecting your energy, or setting a new goal, these actions will compound over time, and they will eventually lead you to the life you've been envisioning.

4. Let Go of Perfectionism

The first page of your comeback story doesn't need to be perfect—it just needs to be written. Perfectionism can hold you back, making you believe that you have to wait until everything is in place before you start. But the reality is, waiting for the perfect moment only keeps you stuck.

Start messy. Start imperfectly. The most important thing is to begin. As you move forward, you'll refine your path, adjust your approach, and grow along the way. But none of that can happen unless you start right now.

Remember, the most successful people didn't wait for the perfect conditions to begin their journeys—they started in the midst of uncertainty, doubt, and imperfection. And they learned, grew, and adapted as they went. You don't need a perfect plan; you need the courage to take that first step.

5. Celebrate Your First Step

As you write the first page of your comeback story, take a moment to celebrate your decision to begin. Acknowledge the bravery it took to step into the unknown. By choosing to start, you've already taken the hardest step. Each day from here forward will be an opportunity to grow, evolve, and continue building your comeback.

Whether it's journaling your thoughts, setting a small goal for the day, or simply taking a deep breath and affirming your commitment to this journey, find a way to honor this first page. You are building momentum, and every small win counts.

Conclusion: The Story Is Yours to Write

Your comeback story is uniquely yours. It's filled with the twists, turns, challenges, and triumphs that only you can experience. And while the first page may feel daunting, it is also a reminder of the incredible power you have to shape your future.

You are not defined by your past mistakes or limitations. You are defined by the choices you make today. By writing the first page of your comeback story, you've taken the first step toward a future full of possibility.

So, what will you write on that first page? Will you write a story of perseverance, strength, and transformation? The pen is in your hands, and the future is waiting for you to create it.

4

The First 30 Days

Detoxing the Mind, Body & Dopamine System

The first 30 days of your semen retention journey can be transformative, but they can also be challenging. One of the most profound aspects of this period is the detoxification process—not just of the body, but also the mind and dopamine system. This detoxification is necessary for you to break free from old habits, reset your energy, and gain control over your impulses. It's a process that requires patience, self-awareness, and commitment, but the rewards—clarity, focus, energy, and resilience—are worth it.

Let's break down how detoxing the mind, body, and dopamine system works and why it's essential for your success.

1. Detoxing the Body: Letting Go of Old Habits

When you first begin the practice of semen retention, your body may react with a mix of physical discomforts and cravings. You may experience heightened urges, restlessness, or a sense of physical tension as your body begins to recalibrate. This is all part of the process. Your body is used to a certain pattern, one that often includes frequent release, and it now has to adjust to a new state of balance.

Detoxing your body during the first 30 days of retention is about clearing out old habits that no longer serve you. These old habits may include patterns of instant gratification, poor diet, lack of exercise, or even self-destructive behaviors that you may have turned to in the past for relief or comfort.

The best way to support your body through this process is by adopting healthy habits that promote balance and vitality. Focus on:

- **Hydration**: Drink plenty of water to flush toxins from your body and keep your system running smoothly.

- **Healthy Diet**: Eat nourishing, whole foods that provide your body with the vitamins and minerals it needs to recover and rebuild. Avoid processed foods and excessive sugar, which can exacerbate cravings and mood swings.

- **Exercise**: Physical activity is essential during this period. It helps to release pent-up energy, reduces stress, and stabilizes your mood. Exercise also boosts your endorphins, helping you feel good without relying on instant gratification.

- **Rest**: Your body needs time to heal and recover, so make sure you're getting enough sleep each night. A well-rested body will be better equipped to handle the detox process and support your retention practice.

As you detox your body, you'll start to feel a shift. The cravings and urges that once seemed all-consuming will begin to lose their grip. Your body will start to crave healthier, more balanced choices, and you'll notice a boost in your overall vitality and energy.

2. Detoxing the Mind: Clearing Mental Clutter

The mental detoxification process is just as crucial as the physical one, especially in the first 30 days. When you've been used to the cycle of constant pleasure-seeking or relying on external stimuli for mental and emotional satisfaction, your mind has developed patterns of dependency. In the case of pornography or excessive sexual release, your mind can become conditioned to rely on these quick hits of dopamine to feel pleasure or escape discomfort.

The first 30 days of semen retention are often filled with mental chatter—old thoughts, old patterns, and even guilt or shame can arise as you break free from these habits. This is the mind detoxing, shedding the old mental attachments that no longer serve you. But it's also an opportunity to clear mental clutter and begin reshaping your thought patterns.

Here's how to support your mental detox during this period:

- **Mindfulness**: Practice mindfulness and meditation to observe your thoughts without judgment. These practices can help you separate from urges, reduce stress, and become more aware of your internal world.

- **Journaling**: Writing can be a powerful tool for mental detoxification. Record your thoughts, feelings, and experiences each day. This will help you process what you're going through and gain clarity about your intentions and progress.

- **Affirmations**: Reinforce positive beliefs about yourself and your journey. Affirmations such as *"I am in control of my energy," "I am becoming stronger every day,"* or *"I am worthy of my goals"* can help retrain your mind to focus on empowerment and growth.

- **Limit Mental Stimulation**: During this time, it's essential to reduce mental clutter. Avoid excessive use of social media, movies, and even negative conversations. Give your mind the space it needs to heal and recalibrate.

The more you engage in these practices, the more you'll begin to experience mental clarity. You'll find that your thoughts become more focused and less dominated by cravings or distractions. Your mind will become sharper, more present, and more capable of handling challenges with calm and strength.

3. Detoxing the Dopamine System: Rewiring for Long-Term Fulfilment

One of the most significant aspects of semen retention is the reset of your dopamine system. Dopamine is the brain's "reward" neurotransmitter, and it's responsible for the feelings of pleasure and satisfaction you experience when engaging in activities like eating, socializing, or sexual release. In today's world, we are constantly bombarded with easy, instant rewards—social media, junk food, pornography—that create a constant surge of dopamine.

When you engage in frequent sexual release or seek instant gratification, your brain becomes accustomed to these rapid dopamine spikes. This can lead to an imbalance, where your brain craves more of these quick rewards, often at the expense of longer-term fulfilment.

The first 30 days of semen retention are critical for resetting your dopamine system. This is where you begin to break free from the cycle of instant gratification and start rewiring your brain for deeper, more meaningful rewards. This process takes time, and you'll experience moments of resistance as your brain adjusts, but it's essential to stay committed.

Here's how to support your dopamine detox during this period:

- **Gradual Reduction of Quick Pleasures**: In addition to semen retention, consider cutting back on other sources of instant gratification, such as excessive screen time, video games, or junk food. This will help your brain learn to find satisfaction in delayed rewards and more fulfilling activities.

- **Pursue Meaningful Goals**: Set long-term goals that require effort and patience to achieve. Whether it's a fitness goal, a creative project, or a personal growth objective, working toward something meaningful will help you rewire your brain to find satisfaction in progress rather than instant pleasure.

- **Practice Delayed Gratification**: Start incorporating small acts of delayed gratification into your daily life. This could be something as simple as waiting a few extra minutes before checking your phone or putting off an indulgence until later in the day. The more you practice this, the stronger your ability to resist immediate urges will become.

Over time, your brain will begin to recalibrate. The constant cravings for instant pleasure will fade, and you'll start to experience greater satisfaction from long-term rewards and achievements. Your dopamine system will become more balanced, and you'll find that the things that truly matter—such as personal growth, meaningful relationships, and long-term success—become more fulfilling than fleeting pleasures.

4. Patience and Persistence

The detox process during the first 30 days can feel intense at times. You might experience physical discomfort, mental restlessness, or emotional turbulence. But remember, this is all part of the process. The discomfort you feel is simply your body and mind shedding old patterns and making way for new, healthier ones.

Be patient with yourself. The first 30 days are a foundation, not a finish line. The changes you make now will set the stage for lasting transformation. Celebrate your progress, no matter how small, and trust that each step you take brings you closer to your goals.

Handling Urges Like a Warrior

In the first 30 days of your semen retention journey, one of the greatest challenges you'll face is managing the powerful urges that arise. Whether it's the urge to release, the desire for instant gratification, or the pull toward old habits, these moments can feel intense and overwhelming. But here's the thing: *every warrior faces battle*. And handling these urges is a test of your discipline, your willpower, and your ability to master your own mind.

Think of each urge as an opportunity—not to give in, but to grow stronger. Like a warrior training for battle, you can face these challenges head-on, learn from them, and ultimately overcome them. The key is to approach them with a mindset of strength and resilience, not fear or shame.

Here's how to handle those urges like a true warrior:

1. Acknowledge the Urge, Don't Fight It

The first step in overcoming any urge is to acknowledge it without judgment. Many people think that in order to succeed with retention, they must avoid the urge altogether or suppress it. But that approach only creates resistance, which ultimately makes the urge stronger. Instead, when an urge arises, simply recognize it for what it is—a passing feeling, not a command.

As a warrior, you don't fight your emotions or urges; you face them with awareness. Say to yourself, *"This is just an urge. It doesn't define me, and it doesn't control me."* By acknowledging the urge and accepting that it's a normal part of the journey, you take away its power. You realize that it's temporary and that you can choose how to respond to it.

2. Shift Your Focus to Something Empowering

A warrior knows that when the battle gets tough, the best strategy is to shift focus to something that fuels them. When you're faced with an urge, don't focus on the urge itself. Instead, redirect your energy toward something empowering—whether that's a physical activity, a productive task, or a mental exercise.

Here are a few ways to shift your focus:

- **Physical Exercise**: One of the most effective ways to deal with urges is to channel that energy into physical activity. Go for a run, do some push-ups, or engage in any exercise that challenges your body. This will help release the pent-up energy, boost your endorphins, and shift your focus away from the temptation.

- **Breathing Exercises**: Focused breathing can help calm your mind and body. Deep breathing exercises, like the 4-7-8 method, can reduce the intensity of the urge and give you a moment of clarity. Inhale deeply for 4 seconds, hold for 7, and exhale for 8. Repeat until you feel more centered.

- **Creative Projects**: Use your surge of energy to create something—whether it's writing, drawing, playing an instrument, or working on a passion project. This channels your energy into something productive and meaningful, rather than letting it get consumed by an urge.

- **Mindfulness or Meditation**: Take a few minutes to center yourself. Close your eyes, breathe deeply, and observe your thoughts without attachment. This practice helps you detach from the urge and recognize that you are not your thoughts—you are the observer of them.

3. Remember Your Vision: Stay Connected to Your Why

The most powerful warriors are driven by a deep sense of purpose. The same is true for you on your retention journey. In the heat of the moment, when an urge feels like it could overtake you, remember *why* you started this path in the first place. Your *why* is your fuel, your source of power, and the foundation of your resolve.

Think back to the vision you created when you defined your *why*—the version of yourself you want to become, the goals you are working toward, and the life you are building. When an urge strikes, pause and remind yourself of your deeper purpose. Reconnect with that vision and let it be the guiding force that helps you make the decision to stay true to your path.

Ask yourself: *Is giving in to this urge aligned with the man I am becoming?* Every time you choose your purpose over short-term pleasure, you reinforce your commitment to the higher version of yourself.

4. Use Visualization as a Tool of Strength

Warriors often use visualization techniques to prepare for battle and envision success. You can do the same with your urges. When you feel an urge coming on, close your eyes and visualize yourself as the person you are striving to be. See yourself strong, calm, and in control of your impulses. Imagine the pride and satisfaction you'll feel at the end of the day, knowing you stayed disciplined and true to your goals.

You can also visualize the urge itself as a wave—a powerful force that rises and falls. See yourself standing firm, unshaken, as the wave crashes over you and then recedes. This imagery reminds you that urges are temporary, and they will pass. You don't need to act on them; you simply need to ride the wave with strength and patience.

5. Embrace the Power of Delayed Gratification

One of the hallmarks of a warrior's mindset is the ability to delay immediate gratification in favor of long-term goals. This is one of the most important lessons you can learn on your retention journey. Every time you resist an urge, you strengthen your ability to delay gratification and build discipline.

When an urge arises, remind yourself that you have the power to choose a delayed reward over immediate pleasure. This is where true mastery lies. By resisting the urge, you're building resilience, mental strength, and emotional control—all of which will serve you far more than a momentary release ever could.

Think about how much more rewarding it will feel to achieve your goals and live with the discipline and clarity you've gained through retention. The longer you wait, the more fulfilling the rewards will be. Your warrior spirit thrives on long-term triumph, not short-lived indulgence.

6. Accept the Battle, but Never Give In

As a warrior, you understand that battles are inevitable, but surrender is not an option. Every urge you face is a battle—but it's one you can win. It's not about never feeling tempted or always being in control; it's about *how* you respond to those moments. A true warrior accepts the challenge, acknowledges it, and uses it as an opportunity to grow stronger.

Each time you successfully handle an urge, you become more resilient. The process of overcoming urges is the training ground for mental toughness and emotional mastery. Over time, you will notice that the urges lose their intensity. You'll have built the discipline to face them without being swayed, and your confidence in your ability to stay in control will grow.

Conclusion: Strength in Every Moment

Handling urges like a warrior is about mental fortitude, patience, and resilience. Every time you face an urge and choose to stay disciplined, you build strength— not just physically, but mentally and emotionally. Remember, urges are a natural part of this journey, but they do not define you. You are the one who defines your actions.

Stay grounded in your purpose, use your mind and body as tools of strength, and continue moving forward with the confidence that you are becoming a warrior who conquers not just the urges, but also the old patterns and limitations that once held you back. With every challenge you overcome, you are one step closer to becoming the best version of yourself.

Replacing Porn: New Habits, New Passions

For many people, porn has become an easy, habitual escape—a quick way to satisfy urges and numb emotions. But as you begin your semen retention journey, one of the most important steps is to replace the old habit with something healthier and more fulfilling. This isn't just about avoiding porn—it's about creating a new lifestyle, one that supports your growth, self-discipline, and inner fulfilment.

This process of replacement is transformative. It's about redirecting the energy once wasted on unhealthy patterns into activities and habits that bring you true joy, purpose, and connection. It's not just about "giving up" something; it's about *gaining* new passions and discovering a deeper sense of satisfaction.

1. Identify the Triggers

Before you can replace porn with new habits, it's essential to identify the triggers that lead to the desire to watch it. Often, porn use is linked to certain emotional states—boredom, loneliness, stress, or the need for a quick dopamine fix. By becoming aware of these triggers, you can begin to create strategies to deal with them in healthier ways.

For example:

- **Boredom**: If you tend to turn to porn when you're bored, this is a clear sign that you need to replace that habit with something engaging. Engage in activities that capture your attention and bring you fulfilment.

- **Stress or Anxiety**: If porn is used as an escape from stress or anxiety, consider incorporating mindfulness practices, breathing exercises, or physical activity into your routine to release tension and promote relaxation.

- **Loneliness**: If porn has been a way to cope with feelings of isolation, this is an opportunity to develop deeper connections with others. Seek out meaningful relationships, spend time with friends, or join communities that align with your interests.

Once you've identified the triggers, you can start to reprogram your mind to associate these moments with healthier alternatives.

2. Create New, Positive Habits

Replacing porn means building new habits—ones that are fulfilling, energizing, and rewarding. The key is to choose activities that align with your values, promote your personal growth, and help you redirect the energy you were previously wasting. Some of these habits might be new, while others may be things you've always wanted to explore but never made the time for.

Here are a few ideas for new habits to replace the old:

- **Exercise and Physical Activity**: One of the best ways to channel the energy that used to go into watching porn is through physical activity. Whether it's hitting the gym, going for a run, practicing yoga, or learning a new sport, exercise boosts your mood, strengthens your body, and provides a natural release of energy and endorphins. Physical fitness is also an excellent way to build confidence and improve your overall well-being.

- **Reading and Personal Development**: Rather than numbing your mind with instant gratification, replace it with books that challenge you and expand your horizons. Whether it's fiction that takes you to new worlds or non-fiction that helps you learn new skills, reading is an enriching habit that nurtures the mind. Use this time to read books on personal development, philosophy, spirituality, or any subject that excites you.

- **Creative Pursuits**: If you've ever had a creative passion that you've put on the back burner, now is the time to revisit it. Whether it's painting, writing, playing an instrument, photography, or something else, engaging in creative activities will not only occupy your mind but also bring a sense of fulfilment and joy. Creativity has the power to elevate your mood and help you express emotions in a healthy, productive way.

- **Learning a New Skill or Hobby**: Sometimes the best way to replace an old habit is to dive into something entirely new. Learn a new language, take up coding, start cooking, or try an instrument. The act of learning something new keeps your mind engaged and gives you a sense of accomplishment.

- **Socializing and Building Meaningful Connections**: If porn has been an outlet for emotional needs, it's important to replace it with deeper, more fulfilling connections with others. Spend time with friends, engage in meaningful conversations, or even explore new social circles. Real relationships can provide the emotional satisfaction and intimacy that porn could never deliver.

3. Build a Morning or Evening Routine

Starting your day with intention can set a positive tone that helps you stay on track. By establishing a morning or evening routine that incorporates healthy habits, you're more likely to stay consistent and feel motivated throughout the day.

For example, your morning routine could include:

- **Meditation or mindfulness** to center yourself

- **Physical exercise** like stretching, yoga, or a quick workout

- **Goal-setting or journaling** to clarify your purpose and intentions for the day

- **Reading or self-improvement** to stimulate your mind

A positive routine gives you a sense of purpose and control, which is crucial in overcoming old habits like porn. It also helps you establish consistency and discipline, making it easier to replace the need for immediate gratification with long-term fulfilment.

4. Find New Sources of Pleasure

One of the most important aspects of replacing porn is rediscovering what truly brings you joy and satisfaction. Porn provides instant pleasure but offers little to no lasting fulfilment. In contrast, building new passions and seeking deeper forms of pleasure will provide you with long-term rewards.

Here are a few ways to rediscover true pleasure:

- **Mindful Enjoyment**: Engage in activities that bring you joy but practice them mindfully. Whether it's eating, listening to music, or spending time in nature, savor the experience rather than rushing through it for instant gratification.

- **Connect with Nature**: Spending time outdoors can be incredibly restorative. Whether it's hiking, biking, or simply taking a walk, being in nature allows you to disconnect from technology and reconnect with yourself. It's also a great way to clear your mind and improve your mood.

- **Self-Care Practices**: Treat yourself with kindness and respect by incorporating regular self-care into your routine. This might include taking a relaxing bath, getting a massage, or simply taking time to rest and recharge.

5. Celebrate Your Progress

Replacing porn is not an easy feat, and it's important to acknowledge your progress along the way. Every day that you choose a new habit over the old one, you are strengthening your willpower and reclaiming your energy. Celebrate these victories, no matter how small they seem.

You can celebrate your progress by:

- **Tracking your success**: Keep a journal where you note how many days you've successfully replaced the urge with something healthier.

- **Rewarding yourself**: Set milestones (e.g., one week, one month) and reward yourself with something meaningful, like a new book, a day trip, or something that aligns with your growth.

6. Patience and Compassion

Changing habits takes time. There will be days when the pull of old patterns feels overwhelming. But remember, the process of replacing porn with healthier habits is a journey, not a destination. Be patient with yourself and don't beat yourself up when you face setbacks. Every day is an opportunity to choose again, and the more you practice, the easier it will become.

Conclusion: A New Path, A New You

Replacing porn with new habits and passions isn't just about getting rid of something negative; it's about creating space for something far more rewarding. As you embark on this journey, you'll find that the energy you once wasted on fleeting pleasure is now channelled into things that truly bring joy, fulfilment, and growth. Embrace this process of transformation with an open heart, knowing that every step you take toward healthier habits is a step toward becoming the best version of yourself.

Would you like to dive deeper into how to sustain these new habits over time or perhaps explore how to integrate these changes into your long-term vision?

Daily Practices: Breathwork, Cold Showers, Meditation

As you move forward on your semen retention journey, it's essential to create a daily routine that nurtures your body, mind, and spirit. The right practices can help you manage urges, build discipline, and foster deeper self-awareness. Three powerful practices that will elevate your energy, strengthen your mind, and support your retention are breathwork, cold showers, and meditation.

These simple but transformative habits will help you stay grounded, centered, and resilient in the face of challenges, while also cultivating a sense of clarity and inner peace. Let's dive into how each of these practices can be a game-changer for your retention journey.

1. Breathwork: Harnessing Your Life Force

Breathing is something we do naturally, but when you bring awareness to your breath, you tap into a powerful tool for emotional regulation, physical energy, and mental clarity. Breathwork can be a game-changer in helping you manage stress, curb urges, and align your energy with your higher goals.

Breathwork helps regulate your nervous system, bringing you into a state of calm and focus, which is especially useful when urges arise. In moments of temptation or stress, conscious breathing can act as a reset, redirecting your focus and calming your mind.

Here are a few effective breathwork techniques to incorporate into your daily routine:

- **Box Breathing (4-4-4-4)**: This technique involves inhaling for 4 seconds, holding your breath for 4 seconds, exhaling for 4 seconds, and holding the breath out for 4 seconds. Box breathing helps calm the nervous system, reduce anxiety, and increase focus.

- **Deep Belly Breathing**: Place one hand on your chest and the other on your stomach. Inhale deeply through your nose, allowing your belly to expand (rather than your chest). Exhale slowly through your mouth. Deep belly breathing helps activate the parasympathetic nervous system, calming your body and improving overall energy.

- **Alternate Nostril Breathing**: Close one nostril with your finger, inhale deeply through the other nostril, and then switch sides. This practice balances the mind, reduces stress, and increases mental clarity.

By starting your day with a few minutes of conscious breathwork, you set a peaceful tone for the hours ahead, reducing the likelihood of giving in to urges or distractions.

2. Cold Showers: Invoking Discipline and Vitality

Cold showers might sound intense, but they are a powerful tool to build mental resilience, increase vitality, and regulate energy levels. When you step into cold water, your body experiences an initial shock, but with consistent practice, this becomes an act of discipline and strength. Cold exposure helps you develop mental toughness by training your mind to remain calm and composed in stressful situations—a valuable skill when you're resisting urges or temptations.

Physically, cold showers stimulate circulation, boost your immune system, and can help increase testosterone levels, which is crucial during your semen retention journey. The cold also triggers the release of endorphins, which improve mood and reduce feelings of stress or anxiety.

Here's how to incorporate cold showers into your daily routine:

- **Start with Warm Water**: Begin your shower with warm water to relax your muscles and ease into the process.

- **Gradually Lower the Temperature**: After a few minutes, begin to reduce the temperature until the water is cold. You don't need to jump straight into freezing water—allow your body to adjust.

- **End with Cold**: Try to end each shower with 30 seconds to 1 minute of cold water. Focus on your breath and stay calm. The key is to embrace the discomfort and breathe through it.

Cold showers not only invigorate your body but also teach you to embrace discomfort and push through resistance—skills that are directly applicable to your retention practice. Over time, you'll notice a greater sense of vitality and energy, which will fuel your commitment to your goals.

3. Meditation: Cultivating Inner Peace and Focus

Meditation is one of the most powerful tools for enhancing self-awareness, clarity, and emotional balance. It helps you build a deeper connection with yourself and gives you the mental space to observe your thoughts without attachment. This is especially valuable when it comes to managing urges and redirecting energy toward positive habits.

Meditation also helps quiet the mind, reducing the noise of stress, anxiety, or distractions that can lead to unhealthy impulses. It trains you to be present in the moment and less reactive to passing thoughts or sensations. By meditating daily, you develop the ability to detach from temporary urges and stay focused on your long-term goals.

Here's how you can begin integrating meditation into your daily routine:

- **Start Small**: Begin with just 5-10 minutes of meditation each morning or evening. As you become more comfortable, you can gradually increase the time.

- **Focus on Your Breath**: One of the simplest meditation techniques is focusing on your breath. Sit in a comfortable position, close your eyes, and bring your attention to the sensation of the breath entering and leaving your body. Whenever your mind wanders, gently guide your focus back to your breath.

- **Body Scan Meditation**: This technique involves mentally scanning your body from head to toe, noticing any areas of tension, discomfort, or relaxation. It helps you become more aware of your physical sensations and cultivates a sense of grounding.

- **Guided Meditation**: If you find it difficult to meditate on your own, you can use guided meditations available through apps like Headspace, Calm, or Insight Timer. These meditations can help you focus on specific goals, such as managing urges or increasing self-discipline.

As you meditate, remember that the goal isn't to "clear your mind" but to observe your thoughts and feelings without judgment. With consistent practice, meditation will help you gain greater control over your mind and strengthen your ability to resist impulsive behaviors.

Conclusion: Strengthen Your Mind, Body, and Spirit

Breathwork, cold showers, and meditation are not just individual practices—they're tools that help you cultivate a powerful, disciplined, and focused mind. By incorporating these practices into your daily routine, you align your body and mind with the goals of semen retention, building resilience and clarity along the way.

The beauty of these practices is that they complement each other. Breathwork calms the mind, cold showers energize the body, and meditation cultivates deep self-awareness. Together, they form a powerful foundation for your retention journey and beyond.

Embrace these daily practices with consistency and patience. Over time, you'll find that not only are you able to manage urges more effectively, but you also feel more grounded, energized, and focused—ready to take on any challenge life throws your way. Would you like to explore other practices that can enhance your retention journey or dive deeper into one of these in particular?

What to Expect: Flatline, Dreams and Early Gains

As you embark on your semen retention journey, it's essential to understand that the process isn't always linear. While it can be incredibly rewarding, it can also come with challenges, especially in the early stages. It's important to approach these phases with patience and awareness, recognizing that they are part of the natural progression toward greater self-mastery and personal growth.

In the first few weeks or months of retention, you'll experience a variety of physical, mental, and emotional changes. Some of these changes will be empowering and motivating, while others may feel like setbacks. Understanding what to expect during this time can help you stay grounded and stay the course.

1. The Flatline: A Temporary Dip in Energy and Motivation

One of the most common experiences during the first phase of semen retention is what's known as the *flatline*. This is a period where your energy, motivation, and mental clarity may seem to drop significantly. You might feel fatigued, lack enthusiasm, or find it harder to stay focused on your goals. It's a frustrating phase, but it's completely normal, and it's often temporary.

Why does this happen?

The flatline is essentially your body and mind adjusting to the absence of the usual dopamine spikes that come from frequent release. In the beginning, your body may go through a sort of recalibration as it shifts from a cycle of instant gratification to a state of sustained energy and clarity. It's important to understand that this flatline phase is part of the healing and resetting process.

Here's how to navigate the flatline:

- **Don't Panic**: This phase is temporary. The initial adjustment period can feel like a slump, but it's a sign that your body and mind are recalibrating. Stay patient and trust the process.

- **Keep Up Your Daily Practices**: Continue engaging in practices like breathwork, meditation, and physical exercise. These will help you push through the flatline by keeping your energy up and focusing your mind on positive, healthy habits.

- **Stay Committed to Your Why**: When motivation feels low, reconnect with your reason for starting this journey. Visualizing the long-term benefits and remembering your deeper purpose will help you keep going, even when things seem harder.

2. Vivid Dreams and Sexual Energy

During the early stages of retention, many people experience an increase in vivid or intense dreams, often involving sexual content. This is a natural part of the process as your body adjusts to holding on to sexual energy instead of releasing it. As you retain your semen, this energy begins to build up in your body and can manifest in your subconscious mind during sleep.

What's happening here?

Semen retention causes a significant shift in your body's hormonal balance, which can influence your sleep patterns and the content of your dreams. It's your body's way of processing the excess energy. Some people report having more frequent, intense, or sexual dreams during the first few weeks or months of retention. This doesn't necessarily mean that you're failing or that your body is "calling for release" in an urgent way; rather, it's a natural process of energy accumulation.

What to do about it:

- **Observe Without Judgment**: Don't judge yourself based on the content of your dreams. It's just your subconscious processing the shift in energy. If these dreams feel unsettling, remind yourself that they are temporary and part of the body's recalibration.

- **Increase Conscious Energy Channeling**: Use the time when you wake up from vivid dreams to focus on grounding techniques—breathwork, meditation, or physical movement. These activities can help channel that energy into something productive, rather than allowing it to overwhelm you.

- **Improve Sleep Hygiene**: Ensure you're getting good quality sleep by maintaining a consistent sleep schedule, creating a calming bedtime routine, and reducing distractions. Quality rest will help reduce the intensity of these dreams over time.

3. Early Gains: Increased Energy, Focus, and Confidence

Despite the challenges of the flatline or vivid dreams, the early stages of semen retention also bring about many positive changes. Once your body adjusts and begins to retain energy consistently, you'll start noticing some of the early gains that come with this practice.

Here are some of the most common early gains you might experience:

- **Increased Energy**: As your body begins to retain sexual energy, you may feel a surge of vitality. You might notice that you're waking up feeling more refreshed, have more stamina throughout the day, and experience fewer energy crashes. This increased energy is often one of the first benefits people report and can motivate you to continue with retention.

- **Mental Clarity**: Many individuals report a significant increase in mental focus and clarity. Without the constant distractions of the brain fog that comes with over-indulgence in instant gratification, you may find it easier to concentrate, make decisions, and stay on track with your goals.

The clarity of mind you gain can be particularly beneficial when it comes to long-term projects, work, or creative endeavors.

- **Emotional Stability**: The fluctuations in mood that often accompany the highs and lows of instant gratification will begin to settle. You'll experience fewer emotional rollercoasters and feel more balanced overall. This emotional stability can help you approach life with greater resilience and calm.

- **Enhanced Confidence**: As you continue your retention journey, many people report feeling more self-assured and empowered. This can manifest as an improved sense of self-worth, greater assertiveness in social situations, and an overall increase in personal confidence. When you no longer rely on external stimuli for validation or pleasure, you begin to trust yourself more deeply.

- **Physical Vitality**: You may also begin to notice subtle physical improvements. This could include clearer skin, improved posture, better digestion, and even an increase in muscle tone, especially if you're combining retention with a healthy lifestyle that includes exercise and proper nutrition.

Conclusion: Navigating the Journey with Patience and Awareness

In the early stages of semen retention, you can expect a mix of challenges and rewards. The flatline, vivid dreams, and early gains are all part of the process that leads to a deeper connection with your energy, your purpose, and yourself. The key is to approach this journey with patience, self-awareness, and a willingness to embrace the ups and downs.

Remember, the flatline is temporary, and the vivid dreams are a natural part of your body adjusting. As you push through these early stages, the gains you experience—physical, mental, and emotional—will make the effort worthwhile. Stay focused on your long-term goals, keep up your daily practices, and trust that the changes you're experiencing are leading you to a more powerful, confident version of yourself. Would you like to explore ways to stay motivated during the flatline or dive deeper into some of the benefits you'll experience later in your retention journey?

5

Energy Rising – Unlocking Vitality & Mental Clarity

Increased Focus, Drive and Discipline

As you continue your semen retention journey, one of the most profound changes you'll begin to notice is an increase in your focus, drive, and discipline. These three attributes are deeply connected, and as you harness your retained energy, they begin to work in synergy to elevate your mental clarity and overall performance in life.

Retention isn't just about abstaining from sexual release; it's about channeling the energy you would have otherwise expended into something far more productive. This energy, once redirected, acts as a powerful fuel for personal growth, helping you to sharpen your focus, ignite your inner drive, and strengthen your sense of discipline. Let's explore each of these elements in detail.

1. Increased Focus: Cutting Through the Noise

One of the most noticeable benefits of semen retention is a marked improvement in your ability to focus. When you are no longer draining your mental energy on impulsive habits or fleeting pleasures, your mind becomes clearer and more receptive to tasks that require attention and concentration. With your energy directed inward, you'll find that distractions no longer pull your attention in a thousand directions.

The process of retention helps you regain control over your thoughts, making it easier to prioritize what matters most. Your brain isn't constantly seeking out dopamine hits from external stimuli, such as social media, porn, or other distractions. Instead, it becomes more efficient, and you develop a natural ability to lock into tasks and complete them with greater precision.

What to Expect:

- **Improved concentration**: Tasks that once seemed tedious or hard to focus on will feel easier to tackle. Whether it's work, studying, or a creative project, you'll find it easier to stay on task.

- **Reduced mental fog**: You'll experience fewer brain fog moments. The clarity that comes with retention allows your mind to function at a higher level, making decisions feel more instinctive.

- **Sharper decision-making**: When your mind is clearer, your decision-making process becomes faster and more confident. You no longer feel overwhelmed by indecision or procrastination.

How to Enhance Your Focus:

- **Practice mindfulness**: Take time each day to practice mindfulness—whether through meditation, focused breathing, or simply being present in the moment. This strengthens your ability to concentrate on the task at hand.

- **Set clear intentions**: Before starting any task, set a clear intention and visualize completing it successfully. This primes your brain to focus on the outcome rather than getting lost in distractions.

2. Increased Drive: Unleashing Your Inner Motivation

As you continue to retain your energy, you'll also experience a dramatic increase in your drive and motivation. Without the constant ebb and flow of dopamine that comes from instant gratification, your brain learns to find motivation from deeper, more meaningful sources. This shift allows you to pursue your goals with a new sense of vigor and determination.

When you no longer rely on external rewards to feel fulfilled, your internal drive takes center stage. You begin to feel an innate pull toward growth, achievement, and improvement. Whether it's advancing in your career, starting a new project, or taking care of your body, your ambition skyrockets as you channel your energy into meaningful pursuits.

What to Expect:

- **A surge in ambition**: You'll notice that you're naturally more motivated to pursue long-term goals. Whether it's building your career, getting in shape, or learning something new, your drive will increase exponentially.

- **Improved work ethic**: You'll feel a stronger internal desire to work hard and stay consistent. Your motivation won't be dependent on external factors, and you'll push yourself to complete tasks with a new sense of purpose.

- **Higher levels of productivity**: With greater drive comes greater productivity. You'll find yourself accomplishing more with less effort, as your energy is focused and directed toward your priorities.

How to Enhance Your Drive:

- **Set meaningful goals**: Define what truly matters to you and create actionable steps toward achieving those goals. This will provide you with a clear sense of direction and purpose.

- **Visualize success**: Spend time each day visualizing yourself achieving your goals. This mental practice will fuel your drive and inspire you to keep pushing forward.

3. Increased Discipline: Mastering Self-Control

Discipline is the backbone of semen retention. When you choose to retain your energy, you are exercising immense self-control. This practice gradually strengthens your ability to resist temptations, stay consistent in your habits, and adhere to your commitments. As you build discipline in one area of your life, it naturally extends to others, creating a domino effect that improves every aspect of your routine.

The increased discipline you gain from retention helps you break free from destructive habits, rewire your brain, and develop healthier, more productive routines. Over time, this sense of discipline becomes second nature. The energy that you once channelled into distractions is now funneled into high-level tasks that push you toward your goals.

What to Expect:

- **Stronger willpower**: As you learn to resist urges, your willpower becomes more resilient. This strengthens your ability to say no to distractions and stay focused on your long-term vision.

- **Better habits**: Retention supports the creation of healthier habits in all areas of life. You'll find yourself gravitating toward productive activities like exercise, reading, and working on your goals, rather than wasting time on fleeting pleasures.

- **Consistency**: As your discipline increases, so does your consistency. You'll be able to show up for yourself every day, even when motivation fluctuates, because your discipline will be the driving force behind your actions.

How to Enhance Your Discipline:

- **Create a structured routine**: Develop a daily schedule that prioritizes your goals. The more structured your day, the less room there is for distractions or procrastination.

- **Start with small wins**: Build your discipline by setting small, achievable goals each day. These small victories will add up over time, making it easier to stay committed to your long-term vision.

- **Track your progress**: Keep a journal or tracker to monitor your journey. This will not only hold you accountable but also allow you to celebrate your progress, reinforcing your commitment to the process.

Conclusion: Rising to New Heights

As your energy rises through semen retention, so too will your ability to focus, drive, and maintain discipline. These qualities are the foundation of personal mastery, and they give you the tools to accomplish whatever you set your mind to. You will feel more capable, more driven, and more empowered as you take ownership of your energy and direct it toward your highest goals.

The transformation you're experiencing isn't just physical—it's mental and emotional as well. Your focus sharpens, your drive intensifies, and your discipline becomes unwavering. These changes will create a ripple effect throughout your life, enabling you to unlock your full potential and achieve new heights of success and fulfilment.

Would you like to dive deeper into how these qualities can impact your specific goals or explore how to maintain this newfound momentum long-term?

How Retention Amplifies Your Work, Workout & Word

Semen retention isn't just about abstaining from sexual release—it's about redirecting and transmuting that vital energy into other areas of your life. As you retain your semen, your energy, focus, and drive intensify, resulting in significant improvements in your work, workouts, and words. These three areas are where the impact of retention is most profoundly felt, as your increased vitality fuels your success and self-expression in ways you might not have imagined.

Let's explore how semen retention can amplify each of these key areas of your life.

1. Retention and Your Work: Increased Focus and Productivity

One of the most immediate and noticeable benefits of semen retention is the boost in focus and mental clarity. Without the constant distractions of low-energy habits, like chasing instant gratification, your mind becomes more aligned with your goals and tasks. This heightened clarity allows you to be far more productive and efficient in your work.

What's happening?

Retention helps recalibrate your brain's chemistry, allowing you to experience higher levels of concentration and mental stamina. With a steady flow of energy and fewer dopamine-driven distractions, you're able to stay deeply immersed in your tasks, problem-solve more effectively, and perform with greater consistency.

What to Expect in Your Work:

- **Sharper Focus**: Your ability to concentrate on complex tasks or long-term projects will increase. No longer distracted by impulses or mental fog, you'll find it easier to work through challenges and finish tasks on time.

- **Enhanced Creativity**: With clearer thoughts and more energy, you'll notice an increase in creative problem-solving and innovative ideas. Retention amplifies your capacity to think outside the box and come up with new solutions.

- **Boosted Efficiency**: As you maintain your energy, you'll find that you need less time to accomplish tasks. You'll be more present, focused, and capable of working at a faster pace, producing higher-quality results with less effort.

How to Maximize Your Work Performance:

- **Prioritize Your Goals**: Use the increased focus from retention to set clear, measurable goals. Break down large tasks into manageable steps to stay on track and prevent overwhelm.

- **Use Your Energy Wisely**: Channel your retained energy into your work. Be mindful of how you use your time, ensuring that you're working on what truly matters and not getting lost in distractions.

2. Retention and Your Workout: Strength and Endurance

Your physical fitness is another area where the benefits of semen retention are immediately felt. Retaining your energy provides you with more stamina, vitality, and strength in the gym or during physical activity. This newfound energy makes it easier to push through workouts, recover faster, and see more significant improvements in your performance.

What's happening?

Retention increases your testosterone levels and boosts the production of other hormones that support muscle growth, endurance, and recovery. This leads to increased strength, more endurance during physical activity, and quicker recovery times after intense exercise. As a result, you'll find yourself performing at higher levels with greater consistency, making faster progress toward your fitness goals.

What to Expect in Your Workout:

- **More Energy and Stamina**: You'll experience a significant increase in endurance during workouts, allowing you to push yourself harder, for longer periods, and with more intensity.

- **Improved Strength**: Retention's impact on hormone levels, particularly testosterone, contributes to better muscle growth and strength. You may notice gains in both strength and muscle mass more rapidly.

- **Faster Recovery**: Retaining energy allows your body to recover quicker from intense physical exertion, leading to less soreness and more frequent training sessions.

How to Maximize Your Workout:

- **Push Yourself**: With your increased energy, now's the time to challenge yourself with more intense workouts or increase the frequency of your training. Use this surge in vitality to reach new physical milestones.

- **Balance Rest and Training**: While your energy may be higher, be mindful of balancing intense workouts with proper rest. Recovery is crucial for muscle growth, and semen retention can enhance your ability to bounce back from even the hardest sessions.

3. Retention and Your Word: Powerful Communication and Confidence

Retention doesn't just improve your physical and mental energy—it also enhances your ability to communicate with confidence and clarity. Whether you're speaking to a colleague, a friend, or an audience, the energy you retain boosts your verbal and non-verbal communication. It helps you speak with greater conviction, express yourself more clearly, and project confidence in every word you say.

What's happening?

As you retain your semen, you begin to tap into a deeper sense of self-awareness and presence. Your thoughts become clearer, and your body language becomes more aligned with your intentions. This enhanced confidence, along with your heightened energy, translates directly into your communication style. People can sense when someone is fully present and confident—and retention empowers you to show up that way.

What to Expect in Your Word:

- **Increased Confidence**: As your energy builds and your mental clarity sharpens, you'll naturally feel more confident in your words. You'll speak with greater authority, whether you're in a professional setting, social situation, or simply having a conversation.

- **Improved Verbal Expression**: You'll notice an increase in your ability to express your thoughts clearly and concisely. Your communication will become more articulate and persuasive, with less fumbling over words.

- **Charisma and Presence**: Retaining energy cultivates a sense of personal magnetism that makes you more charismatic and compelling in conversations. People will naturally be drawn to you because of your grounded, confident energy.

How to Maximize Your Communication:

- **Be Present**: Whether in meetings, social gatherings, or one-on-one conversations, be fully present. Use the energy you've retained to engage deeply with those around you, making them feel heard and valued.

- **Practice Assertiveness**: Use your newfound confidence to speak up and express your thoughts, ideas, and boundaries clearly. Assertiveness is key to building respect in your personal and professional life.

Conclusion: The Power of Retention in Every Area of Your Life

Semen retention is a powerful tool for amplifying every area of your life—especially your work, workouts, and words. As your energy rises, you'll find that your mental clarity, physical stamina, and communication skills all improve in tandem, creating a synergistic effect that elevates your performance across the board.

Retention empowers you to work with more focus and productivity, push your physical limits and recover more quickly, and speak with greater confidence and presence. The key is to stay committed to the practice and channel your retained energy into meaningful action in all aspects of your life.

By integrating these improvements into your daily routine, you'll unlock your true potential and experience a powerful transformation that touches every area of your being.

Would you like to explore how you can maintain momentum in these areas or dive deeper into strategies for specific goals?

Cleaning Up Your Life: Diet, Environment, Relationships

As you continue on your semen retention journey, it's crucial to recognize that your environment—both internal and external—plays a significant role in your progress. Just as retaining your energy gives you a boost in focus, drive, and discipline, cleaning up your life in terms of your diet, surroundings, and relationships will enhance the effects of retention and create a positive, supportive space for growth. By making conscious improvements in these areas, you align your body and mind with your new purpose, ensuring that every aspect of your life is working in harmony.

Let's explore how cleaning up these three vital areas—diet, environment, and relationships—can elevate your energy, boost your results, and help you fully embrace the power of retention.

1. Diet: Fuelling Your Body with Purpose

What you eat directly affects the quality of your energy, mental clarity, and overall well-being. When you practice semen retention, your body and mind are in a state of transformation, and fueling yourself with the right foods will maximize your results. A healthy, clean diet provides the nutrients needed to sustain your energy levels, optimize hormone production, and support physical and mental clarity.

What's happening?

Certain foods can either drain or boost your energy, depending on their nutritional value. A diet high in processed foods, sugar, and unhealthy fats can leave you feeling sluggish, mentally foggy, and physically drained. On the other hand, whole, nutrient-dense foods provide the building blocks your body needs to thrive and support your retention efforts. A clean, balanced diet will help your body produce more testosterone naturally, maintain optimal brain function, and keep your energy levels consistent throughout the day.

What to Focus On:

- **Whole Foods**: Prioritize fresh, whole foods like vegetables, fruits, lean proteins, whole grains, and healthy fats. These provide the vitamins, minerals, and nutrients your body needs to fuel itself.

- **High-Quality Protein**: Protein-rich foods like eggs, fish, chicken, legumes, and plant-based proteins support muscle growth, tissue repair, and hormone production.

- **Healthy Fats**: Include sources of healthy fats, such as avocados, nuts, seeds, and olive oil. These fats help support brain health, hormone regulation, and long-lasting energy.

- **Hydration**: Drinking plenty of water is essential for maintaining optimal mental and physical function. Hydration helps with focus, energy levels, and digestion.

- **Avoid Processed Foods**: Limit your intake of processed, sugary foods and artificial additives. These can lead to energy crashes, brain fog, and inflammation, hindering your progress.

How to Maximize Your Diet:

- **Plan Your Meals**: Preparing balanced meals in advance ensures that you're consistently fueling your body with the right nutrients.

- **Eat Mindfully**: Pay attention to what you're eating and how it makes you feel. Eating mindfully helps you make better food choices and prevents overeating.

2. Environment: Creating a Space That Supports Your Growth

The environment you surround yourself with has a profound impact on your energy levels, mindset, and ability to stay focused. A cluttered, chaotic environment can contribute to stress, distractions, and mental fatigue, while a clean, organized, and positive environment can enhance your sense of peace, clarity, and motivation.

What's happening?

When you practice retention, your energy becomes more sensitive and powerful. It's essential to ensure that your physical environment supports your growth and aligns with your higher goals. A clean and organized space promotes mental clarity and focus, while an environment filled with negativity or distractions can drain your energy and hinder your progress.

What to Focus On:

- **Declutter**: Start by decluttering your space. Whether it's your home, workspace, or even digital devices, removing physical and mental clutter helps reduce distractions and creates a sense of calm.

- **Create a Productive Space**: Set up areas that promote productivity, whether it's a clean desk, a meditation corner, or a workout space. Surround yourself with items that inspire you, such as motivational quotes, artwork, or meaningful objects.

- **Surround Yourself with Nature**: Nature has a grounding and calming effect on the mind and body. If possible, spend time outdoors, or bring elements of nature inside, like plants or natural light.

- **Reduce Negative Energy**: Be mindful of the media you consume and the company you keep. Avoid watching content that drains your energy or fills your mind with negativity, and choose to spend time with people who lift you up and encourage your growth.

How to Maximize Your Environment:

- **Create Rituals**: Set up daily rituals in your space that help you focus, relax, or recharge, such as morning stretches, journaling, or quiet reflection.

- **Keep Your Space Clean**: Regularly tidy your environment to keep it clear of distractions. A clean, organized space supports a clear mind and promotes productivity.

3. Relationships: Surrounding Yourself with Positivity

The people you associate with can have a huge impact on your energy, mindset, and emotional health. Relationships, both positive and negative, directly influence how you feel and how effectively you can focus on your goals. When you engage in healthy, supportive relationships, your energy is uplifted, your confidence is strengthened, and you are encouraged to continue your path of growth. Conversely, toxic relationships can drain your energy, create unnecessary stress, and lead you off course.

What's happening?

As you practice retention, your energy becomes more sensitive, and your emotional state is more reflective of the people around you. Spending time with individuals who share your values, support your growth, and encourage your well-being can help you stay aligned with your goals. On the other hand, spending time with negative, critical, or unsupportive people can leave you feeling drained, insecure, and unmotivated.

What to Focus On:

- **Seek Positive Connections**: Build relationships with people who encourage and uplift you. Surround yourself with those who share your values, challenge you to grow, and celebrate your successes.

- **Let Go of Toxic Relationships**: Recognize when certain relationships are no longer serving you. Toxic relationships can undermine your progress, so it's important to set boundaries or distance yourself from people who drain your energy.

- **Strengthen Emotional Support Systems**: Cultivate relationships that provide emotional support and understanding. Whether it's a mentor, close friend, or partner, having people you trust around you can help you stay motivated and resilient.

How to Maximize Your Relationships:

- **Communicate Openly**: Build trust and understanding with the people in your life by being open and honest about your needs, goals, and boundaries.

- **Set Healthy Boundaries**: Protect your energy by setting clear boundaries in your relationships. Don't be afraid to say no to situations or people that drain you or distract you from your purpose.

- **Cultivate Meaningful Connections**: Focus on deepening the quality of your relationships rather than the quantity. Invest in connections that bring you joy, fulfilment, and support.

Conclusion: A Holistic Approach to Growth

Cleaning up your life is an essential part of the semen retention journey. By optimizing your diet, environment, and relationships, you create the ideal conditions for your energy to rise and your goals to be realized. When you consciously choose to fuel your body with nourishing foods, surround yourself with positivity, and engage in relationships that support your growth, you accelerate your transformation and unlock your full potential.

Remember, semen retention is not just about holding onto energy—it's about creating a lifestyle that aligns with your highest values and supports your personal growth. By making these small but powerful changes in your life, you'll amplify the benefits of retention and take your vitality, focus, and confidence to new heights.

Would you like more tips on how to implement these changes in your life or dive deeper into any of these areas?

Sexual Transmutation: Using Energy Creatively

Sexual energy is one of the most powerful forces within the human body. Traditionally, it is often seen as something that can only be used for reproduction or sexual pleasure. However, when you practice semen retention, you begin to understand that this energy can be harnessed and transmuted into something much greater—a source of creativity, drive, and personal power.

Sexual transmutation is the process of redirecting sexual energy into creative, productive, and meaningful pursuits. Rather than allowing this energy to dissipate or be squandered in fleeting pleasures, transmutation channels it into endeavors that enhance your life, such as work, artistic expression, physical fitness, or intellectual pursuits.

The key to sexual transmutation is the realization that the energy that would have otherwise been spent in a physical release is now available to fuel your passions, ideas, and ambitions. By learning how to direct this energy purposefully, you can tap into a well of creativity and vitality that will propel you forward in every area of life.

1. The Power of Sexual Energy

Sexual energy is, at its core, life energy. It is a force that sustains creation and drives us to connect with others and the world around us. When you retain your semen, this energy doesn't simply disappear—it gets stored in your body, waiting

85

to be transmuted. It becomes an internal fuel source that can be redirected toward any goal or project that requires focus, inspiration, or motivation.

This energy is deeply connected to your creativity. When you stop releasing it, you allow it to build up and intensify within you, which in turn enhances your mental clarity and emotional resilience. This surge of energy can give you the drive and insight to embark on new projects, solve complex problems, or push through creative blocks.

2. How to Transmute Sexual Energy

Sexual transmutation is a conscious act of channeling your energy from the base instincts of pleasure and desire to higher-level creative and productive outlets. It's about using your energy to create something meaningful, whether it's a work of art, a business idea, or an athletic achievement.

Here's how to begin transmuting sexual energy:

- **Channel it into your work**: Rather than allowing sexual urges to distract you, use that energy to fuel your focus and productivity. If you're working on a project, break through mental barriers by redirecting your attention to the task at hand. You'll find that your output increases, and your ability to focus becomes sharper.

- **Tap into your creativity**: Use the energy to enhance your creative endeavors. Whether it's painting, writing, playing music, or crafting something new, the energy stored from retention can fuel your creativity and unlock new levels of expression. Many artists, writers, and musicians have reported that sexual energy is an essential part of their creative process.

- **Physical activities**: Channel sexual energy into your workouts, sports, or physical challenges. The surge of energy and vitality from retention can make you more driven and capable in the gym or during any athletic activity. You'll notice increased strength, stamina, and endurance as you push your physical limits.

- **Meditation and Visualization**: Transmutation also involves elevating your energy to a higher level of consciousness. Practice meditation to refine your focus and clarity. During your practice, visualize your goals and imagine using your energy to bring them into reality. This helps reinforce the connection between your retained energy and your desired outcomes.

3. The Creative Power of Retained Energy

When you transmute sexual energy, you create a positive feedback loop. The more energy you channel into your creative pursuits, the more productive and inspired you become. As you begin to accomplish your goals, the sense of fulfilment and success fuels further retention, and the cycle continues.

Sexual energy is inherently connected to creation, and by redirecting it toward your creative pursuits, you can manifest new opportunities, ideas, and projects in your life. It allows you to step into a higher level of self-expression and personal achievement.

What to Expect:

- **Increased innovation**: The creative breakthroughs that come from transmuting your sexual energy can open doors to new ideas and innovations. Whether you're in a field that requires constant problem-solving or are trying to create something artistic, the surge of energy can provide the spark you need.

- **Enhanced focus**: As your energy is redirected, you may notice that distractions diminish, and your ability to focus on your long-term goals intensifies. You become less impulsive and more determined to succeed.

- **Heightened passion and drive**: By channeling your energy into projects that excite you, you'll feel a deeper sense of passion and commitment. This drive will keep you on track even during challenging times, helping you push through obstacles with a sense of purpose.

4. A Holistic Approach to Transmutation

Sexual transmutation is not just about redirecting energy into your work or creative activities—it's about cultivating a holistic sense of balance and vitality in your life. When you retain your sexual energy, you begin to take control over how you direct your life force. You become more mindful of your time, energy, and focus, ensuring that every part of your life is contributing to your growth.

It's important to note that transmutation isn't about repressing or denying your desires—it's about elevating them. Instead of allowing yourself to be enslaved by fleeting pleasures, you transform the raw energy of desire into something more meaningful and fulfilling.

5. The Results of Successful Transmutation

When you successfully practice sexual transmutation, you'll notice a range of benefits that manifest both physically and mentally. Your energy levels will remain high, your creativity will flourish, and your ability to stay focused on your goals will improve. You'll become more disciplined and proactive in all areas of your life.

The long-term effects of transmutation include:

- **Increased productivity** and effectiveness in your work

- **Greater satisfaction** in your creative projects and personal achievements

- **More harmonious relationships** as you become more emotionally balanced and confident

- **A deeper connection** to your purpose and the ability to manifest your desires

Conclusion: Embracing the Creative Potential of Your Sexual Energy

Sexual transmutation allows you to tap into a hidden well of creative potential that exists within you. By redirecting your sexual energy into productive and meaningful pursuits, you unlock your ability to perform at your best, achieve your goals, and express yourself in ways that are deeply fulfilling. Whether you're building your career, creating art, or strengthening your body, semen retention provides the fuel that powers your most ambitious and creative endeavors.

Embrace this transformative process, and use your sexual energy not just for momentary pleasure but as a force that propels you toward personal mastery, success, and self-expression. The key is to consciously channel your energy into what truly matters, and in doing so, you'll discover just how powerful and limitless your potential can be.

Are you ready to begin using your sexual energy creatively, and if so, which area of your life would you like to focus your energy on first?

Rewiring the Brain for Long-Term Change

The journey of semen retention is more than just a physical or emotional challenge—it's a mental one. As you take steps to transmute your sexual energy, improve your focus, and embrace new habits, you're also rewiring your brain. This process involves breaking old patterns, forming new neural connections, and creating lasting, positive change that will support your goals and growth for the long term.

Our brains are incredibly adaptable, and the habits we cultivate shape how we think, behave, and respond to the world. This phenomenon, known as **neuroplasticity**, means that the more we practice a particular behavior or mindset, the more it becomes ingrained in our neural networks. When you embark on the path of semen retention and consciously direct your energy, you're essentially training your brain to think differently, act more intentionally, and overcome the habits and impulses that once controlled you.

Let's explore how you can use this process of rewiring your brain to create lasting change.

1. Breaking Old Habits: Overcoming the Past

One of the first steps in rewiring your brain is breaking free from old, limiting habits. This is particularly important when it comes to behaviors like watching porn, compulsive sexual release, or seeking instant gratification. These habits form powerful neural pathways in the brain that create automatic responses to stress, boredom, or desire.

When you begin practicing semen retention, you're consciously choosing to break these pathways and replace them with healthier, more productive behaviors. The initial resistance may feel strong, but with consistent effort, the old pathways begin to weaken, and new ones start to form. Over time, the urges and cravings you once felt will lose their power, as your brain adapts to the new patterns you're reinforcing.

How to Break Old Habits:

- **Identify Triggers**: Pay attention to the moments or emotions that prompt your old habits. Once you identify your triggers, you can begin to avoid or transform them into opportunities for growth.

- **Replace with Positive Actions**: Instead of allowing yourself to fall into old patterns, replace them with healthier alternatives. For example, when you feel the urge to release, you might engage in physical activity, meditation, or deep breathing to redirect that energy.

- **Be Patient**: Rewiring your brain takes time. Don't be discouraged by occasional setbacks—continue to practice your new habits consistently, and you'll notice gradual, lasting change.

2. Building New Neural Pathways: The Power of Consistency

Rewiring the brain for long-term change doesn't happen overnight. It requires patience, consistency, and commitment. Every time you practice semen retention and consciously channel your energy into productive activities—whether that's work, physical exercise, creative pursuits, or spiritual growth—you are reinforcing new neural pathways that strengthen your ability to focus, resist temptation, and act in alignment with your goals.

The more you practice these new behaviors, the more automatic they will become. This is because your brain will begin to prioritize the new pathways over the old ones. In time, the positive actions you've taken will feel more natural and less effortful, creating a foundation for long-term success.

How to Build New Neural Pathways:

- **Consistency is Key**: The more frequently you engage in your new habits, the more your brain will adapt. Small, consistent efforts add up to big changes over time.

- **Celebrate Progress**: Acknowledge every milestone, whether it's going one day without giving in to urges or successfully transmuting your energy into a creative project. Celebrating small wins reinforces the positive neural pathways and strengthens your resolve.

- **Stay Committed**: Remain committed even when the going gets tough. Every time you choose to resist old patterns and embrace new behaviors, you are rewiring your brain for long-term success.

3. Overcoming Resistance: Managing Urges and Emotions

As you work to rewire your brain, you will encounter resistance. This resistance often comes in the form of cravings, urges, or emotional challenges. These sensations arise because your brain is still accustomed to old patterns that seek quick gratification. However, with practice, you can train your brain to manage these urges in a healthier way.

When you experience resistance, it's important to remember that this is simply part of the rewiring process. It's a sign that your brain is adapting and challenging its old habits. The key is to remain patient and compassionate with yourself while you strengthen your new pathways.

How to Manage Resistance:

- **Mindfulness**: When you feel urges or emotional resistance, practice mindfulness. Instead of reacting impulsively, pause and observe your thoughts and feelings. Acknowledge them without judgment and allow them to pass.

- **Emotional Regulation**: Learn how to regulate your emotions without relying on quick fixes like pornography or sexual release. Techniques such as deep breathing, journaling, or engaging in physical activities can help you stay grounded and in control.

- **Reframe Negative Thoughts**: When you experience doubts or negative self-talk, reframe those thoughts. Instead of thinking, "I can't do this," try thinking, "I am rewiring my brain for success, and every challenge is an opportunity for growth."

4. Creating Long-Term Change: Aligning Mind and Body

Long-term change comes when you align your mind, body, and actions with your new purpose. Rewiring your brain isn't just about mental effort—it's also about physical energy. As you practice semen retention, you're harnessing your life force and directing it toward positive outcomes, which in turn strengthens your mental and emotional resilience. Your body becomes the vessel for your new habits, and your mind becomes the driver.

To create lasting change, you must reinforce this alignment by consistently making choices that support your new habits, whether it's maintaining a clean diet, engaging in regular exercise, or cultivating healthy relationships. When your actions align with your new mindset, you solidify the neural connections that support your growth.

How to Create Long-Term Change:

- **Establish Healthy Routines**: Build routines that support your physical, emotional, and mental well-being. Start each day with intention, setting the tone for a productive and positive mindset.

- **Set Clear Intentions**: Stay connected to your "why" and regularly remind yourself of the goals and values you are working toward. Clear intentions help guide your actions and keep you on track.

- **Balance and Adaptability**: As you rewire your brain, don't forget to allow room for flexibility and adaptation. Life is dynamic, and being able to adjust while staying true to your core values will ensure sustainable growth.

5. The Power of Time and Persistence

Lastly, remember that rewiring the brain is a gradual process. The brain is constantly evolving, and change requires time and persistent effort. Over weeks, months, and even years, your old habits will lose their grip, and the new pathways will grow stronger. The rewards of this process are lasting, bringing you a sense of mental clarity, emotional stability, and enhanced creativity.

With each day that you stay committed to your practice of semen retention and channel your energy into positive outlets, you'll reinforce the new version of yourself. This is the power of neuroplasticity: the brain's ability to adapt and grow based on your intentional actions.

Conclusion: Rewiring for a New You

Rewiring your brain for long-term change is the key to making your semen retention practice truly transformative. By breaking old patterns, building new neural pathways, and aligning your mind, body, and actions, you create a powerful foundation for lasting growth. Over time, these changes become ingrained in who you are, and you'll notice yourself becoming more focused, disciplined, creative, and in control of your life.

This journey requires patience, but the results are more than worth it. As you continue to practice and reinforce your new habits, your brain will adapt, your desires will shift, and you'll become the best version of yourself—living with greater clarity, energy, and purpose.

Are you ready to embrace the long-term changes that come with rewiring your brain and taking control of your future?

6

Reclaiming Masculinity

Rebuilding Self-Esteem from the Inside Out

Self-esteem is the foundation upon which everything else in your life is built. It's the lens through which you see yourself, the world, and your potential. Yet, for many men, self-esteem becomes a casualty of negative experiences, external pressures, and internal struggles. Whether it's from societal expectations, past failures, or the habits we've formed over time, many of us find our sense of worth eroded.

Reclaiming your masculinity begins with rebuilding self-esteem from the inside out. This process isn't about external validation or quick fixes—it's about cultivating a deep, unwavering belief in your own value, regardless of what's happening around you. True self-esteem is rooted in self-awareness, self-acceptance, and self-love. It's about recognizing your intrinsic worth and taking responsibility for your own growth.

Here's how you can begin to rebuild your self-esteem and reclaim your sense of masculinity:

1. Recognize Your Worth

The first step in rebuilding your self-esteem is to truly understand your value—not based on external achievements or approval, but as a person in your own right. You are worthy simply because you exist. Many men struggle with feelings of inadequacy because they tie their self-worth to their accomplishments, relationships, or how others perceive them. But the foundation of true self-esteem comes from knowing, deep down, that you matter.

This means recognizing the unique qualities, strengths, and potential you possess. It's important to take a moment each day to acknowledge your achievements—no matter how small—and to affirm your worth in ways that go beyond your output or external validation.

How to Recognize Your Worth:

- **Affirmations**: Start your day with positive affirmations. Speak to yourself kindly and acknowledge your strengths. Remind yourself of the things you're proud of and the qualities that make you unique.

- **Self-Reflection**: Take time to reflect on your past successes and the qualities that have allowed you to overcome obstacles. Celebrate your resilience, determination, and growth.

- **Self-Compassion**: Treat yourself with the same compassion you would offer a close friend. Instead of berating yourself for mistakes or perceived shortcomings, practice kindness and patience as you work through challenges.

2. Challenge Negative Self-Talk

The internal dialogue we carry with ourselves plays a massive role in shaping our self-esteem. Many men are their own harshest critics, holding themselves to unattainable standards and constantly comparing themselves to others. This negative self-talk can be a powerful barrier to rebuilding self-esteem.

To reclaim your masculinity and rebuild your sense of self-worth, it's crucial to challenge these negative thoughts and replace them with healthier, more empowering perspectives. Start by becoming aware of when you're engaging in self-criticism or unproductive thoughts, and then consciously redirect those thoughts in a positive direction.

How to Challenge Negative Self-Talk:

- **Mindfulness**: Practice mindfulness to become aware of your inner dialogue. When negative thoughts arise, pause and assess their validity. Ask yourself, "Is this thought helpful?" or "Would I say this to someone I care about?"

- **Reframe Your Thoughts**: Instead of thinking, "I'm not good enough," reframe it to "I'm doing my best, and I'm improving every day." Replace self-criticism with constructive thoughts that support your growth.

- **Journaling**: Write down your thoughts and feelings as a way to gain perspective. Journaling helps you process emotions and identify patterns of negative thinking that can be challenged and reframed.

3. Build Physical Confidence

The way you feel about your body can have a profound impact on your self-esteem. When you take care of your physical health—whether it's through exercise, healthy eating, or improved hygiene—you send a powerful message to your mind: *You are worth the effort.* This doesn't mean striving for a perfect body, but rather cultivating a sense of pride and respect for your physical self.

Regular exercise is one of the best ways to improve both physical and mental health. Not only does it increase your physical strength and endurance, but it also releases endorphins—natural mood boosters—that help build mental resilience and confidence. As you begin to see improvements in your fitness, you'll feel more empowered and more connected to your masculinity.

How to Build Physical Confidence:

- **Exercise Regularly**: Incorporate physical activity into your daily routine. Whether it's strength training, yoga, running, or sports, exercise helps to improve your body, boost your energy, and elevate your mood.

- **Prioritize Health**: Focus on nourishing your body with wholesome food, staying hydrated, and getting enough sleep. A healthy body promotes a healthy mind.

- **Posture**: Pay attention to your posture. Standing tall with your shoulders back and your head held high can make a significant difference in how you feel about yourself and how others perceive you.

4. Set and Achieve Meaningful Goals

Self-esteem is reinforced through action. When you set meaningful goals and take steps to achieve them, you prove to yourself that you are capable and deserving of success. These goals don't have to be monumental; even small, incremental achievements build confidence over time.

Start by identifying goals that align with your values and passions. Whether they're related to your career, personal development, relationships, or hobbies, having something to strive for provides a sense of purpose and accomplishment.

How to Set and Achieve Meaningful Goals:

- **Set SMART Goals**: Make sure your goals are specific, measurable, attainable, relevant, and time-bound. Break them down into manageable steps to avoid feeling overwhelmed.

- **Track Progress**: Keep track of your progress, and celebrate small wins along the way. This helps reinforce the belief that you are capable of achieving whatever you set your mind to.

- **Learn from Setbacks**: Understand that setbacks are part of the process. Instead of letting failures define you, see them as learning opportunities that help you grow.

5. Surround Yourself with Positive Influences

The people we spend time with greatly influence how we feel about ourselves. To rebuild your self-esteem, it's essential to surround yourself with individuals who uplift, support, and encourage your growth. Toxic relationships or negative environments only reinforce feelings of inadequacy and self-doubt.

Choose to engage with people who respect and value you, and distance yourself from those who drain your energy or belittle your worth. Positive relationships are an important part of nurturing a healthy self-esteem, as they provide the encouragement and validation that supports your journey.

How to Surround Yourself with Positive Influences:

- **Seek Uplifting Relationships**: Cultivate relationships with people who share your values and who inspire you to be your best self. Supportive friends, mentors, or a strong community can help reinforce your sense of worth.

- **Set Boundaries**: Protect your energy by setting boundaries with individuals who are toxic or consistently negative. Your self-esteem deserves to be nurtured in environments that are positive and supportive.

- **Be Your Own Best Friend**: Sometimes, the most important relationship is the one you have with yourself. Practice self-love and be kind to yourself, even in the face of mistakes or setbacks.

Conclusion: Owning Your Masculinity

Rebuilding self-esteem from the inside out is the cornerstone of reclaiming your masculinity. By recognizing your worth, challenging negative self-talk, building physical confidence, achieving meaningful goals, and surrounding yourself with positive influences, you begin to reshape how you see yourself. This process isn't quick or easy, but it's essential for stepping into your full power as a man.

True masculinity isn't about conforming to rigid societal expectations or seeking external validation. It's about owning your own identity, understanding your value, and standing confidently in who you are. As you rebuild your self-esteem, you not only reclaim your masculinity—you create the foundation for a life filled with purpose, self-respect, and fulfilment.

Are you ready to begin the process of rebuilding your self-esteem, and in doing so, reclaim the powerful, authentic man you are meant to be?

Confidence Without Ego

There's a kind of confidence that doesn't need to shout. It doesn't puff its chest or demand attention. It just *is*—quiet, steady, and powerful. That's the kind of confidence we're talking about here. Not the loud kind that's built on ego. But the grounded kind that comes from truly knowing yourself.

Too often, we mistake ego for strength. We think being confident means being the loudest voice in the room, the toughest guy at the table, or the one with all the answers. But ego is a mask. It's armor we wear when we're afraid of being seen too clearly.

Real confidence doesn't come from how others see you. It comes from how you see yourself—when no one's watching. It's born from self-respect, not self-importance. It's the quiet power of a man who knows what he stands for, even if no one else claps for him.

To reclaim your masculinity is to return to that kind of confidence. One that doesn't need to prove anything. One that allows space for humility, for listening, for presence. It's not afraid to admit when it's wrong. It's not shaken by other people's opinions.

Ego says, *"Look at me."* Confidence says, *"I see myself."*

There's freedom in this. You no longer have to perform or pretend. You just show up. Fully. Honestly. And that, more than anything, is what makes people trust you, respect you, and follow you.

Let go of the need to impress. Trust in who you are. That's where true masculine power lives. Not in ego, but in essence. Not in dominance, but in depth.

And the best part? That kind of confidence never runs out—because it's not borrowed from the outside. It's built from within.

Restoring Honor, Boundaries & Integrity

There was a time when a man's word meant something. When honor wasn't just an idea—it was how you lived. Today, in a world full of distractions, quick wins, and blurred lines, we've drifted from that place. But it's not lost. You can come back to it. And when you do, everything changes.

Honor starts with how you treat yourself. Not in public, but in private. Do you keep the promises you make to yourself? Do you show up when no one else is watching? That's where integrity is forged—not in grand gestures, but in the small daily choices that add up to a life you can be proud of.

Boundaries are part of this. They're not walls—they're lines drawn from self-respect. They say: *This is what I allow. This is what I protect. This is who I am.* Setting boundaries isn't weakness. It's leadership. It's the ability to say no without guilt, and yes without losing yourself.

When you restore boundaries, you restore direction. You stop leaking energy into things that don't serve your purpose. You stop betraying yourself to please others. And that creates space—for clarity, for peace, for strength.

Integrity is what ties it all together. It's alignment between your words, your actions, and your values. It's not about being perfect—it's about being real. Owning your mistakes. Making things right when you fall short. Walking your talk, even when it's inconvenient. This is what it means to be grounded in true masculinity. Not control. Not ego. But honor. Boundaries. Integrity.

When a man stands in that, people feel it. They trust him. They're drawn to him—not because he's trying to prove anything, but because he's *become* something solid. And the truth is, the world doesn't need more tough guys. It needs more men of honor.

Start there. Begin with yourself. And let everything else follow.

The Retained Man vs. The Drained Man

There are two kinds of men in this world: the *Retained Man* and the *Drained Man*.

The *Drained Man* is everywhere. You've seen him—tired in the eyes, scattered in the mind, disconnected from purpose. He's always chasing, always giving his energy away to things that don't feed him: endless scrolling, cheap pleasure, approval from others, relationships that take but never give back. He might look busy, even successful on the outside, but inside? He's empty. He's burned out. He's leaking life force by the hour, and he doesn't even know it.

Then there's the *Retained Man*. You can feel his presence when he walks into a room. He's calm, not because life is easy—but because he's in control of his energy. He doesn't give himself away freely. He chooses where his time, attention, and power go. He protects what's sacred. He doesn't spill his essence to escape discomfort—he holds it, refines it, and uses it to build something greater.

This isn't just about physical retention—it's mental, emotional, spiritual. The *Retained Man* doesn't let anger control him. He doesn't react to every opinion, every temptation. He knows his value. He knows his mission. And because of that, he walks differently. Talks differently. Loves differently.

The difference between these two men isn't talent, or luck, or circumstance. It's discipline. It's awareness. It's choice.

The *Drained Man* says yes to everything—and loses himself in the noise. The *Retained Man* says yes to what aligns—and no to what distracts. One is ruled by impulse. The other is guided by intention. One ends the day exhausted and uncertain. The other ends the day with fuel left in the tank, clarity in his mind, and purpose in his heart.

Every day, you get to choose which man you'll be. You don't have to be perfect. You just have to be present. So ask yourself: Am I retaining my power? Or am I draining it? Because the man you become tomorrow starts with how you answer that today.

Women and Attraction: A Byproduct, Not the Goal

Let's clear something up: women are not the goal. Attraction is not the mission.

It's a *byproduct*—a natural result of becoming the man you were meant to be. Too many men move through life trying to earn attention, trying to impress, trying to mold themselves into whatever they think will make them desirable. But that's backwards. That's chasing, and chasing always leads to frustration, burnout, and disappointment.

Here's the truth: when you're dialled in—when you're living with purpose, walking in integrity, building your life brick by brick—attraction just *happens*. Not because you're trying to be someone, but because you *are* someone.

A man grounded in who he is doesn't have to convince anyone of his worth. He doesn't need tricks, games, or strategies. He doesn't need to manipulate attention—he *commands* it, without even trying. That kind of presence is magnetic. It's rare. And women feel it.

But here's the deeper part: when women become the goal, you lose yourself. You shape-shift. You perform. You start outsourcing your value to how someone else sees you. And that's not power. That's dependence dressed up as desire. Real masculinity is about creating a life that *pulls* the right things toward you—without needing to chase any of them. It's about choosing the kind of woman who aligns with your mission, not sacrificing your mission to win her over. So stop asking, *"How do I attract her?"* Start asking, *"Am I proud of the man I'm becoming?"*

Because when your life is rooted in purpose, when your energy is clean, when your mind is clear and your actions are consistent—attraction becomes effortless. Natural. Organic. It's not the prize. It's the echo. Build the man. And let the rest follow.

7

Living High Vibe

Frequency & Energy: What You Emit, You Attract

Everything is energy. You've heard that before—but really let it sink in. Every thought you think, every word you speak, every action you take is sending out a frequency. Like a signal. And the world responds to that signal. Not always instantly, but always accurately.

This is why your energy matters more than you realize. You attract what you *are*, not what you pretend to be. If you carry frustration, scarcity, or insecurity, the world will mirror that back to you. You'll pull in chaos, resistance, and relationships that match the noise inside you. That's not punishment—it's feedback.

But when you start shifting your internal frequency—when you operate from peace, clarity, gratitude, and purpose—you begin to attract different experiences. Better ones. Aligned ones. Not because you're lucky, but because your vibration invites them in.

Think of it like a radio. You can't tune into a jazz station if you're stuck on heavy metal. If you want peace, you have to *broadcast* peace. If you want abundance, you have to *embody* abundance. If you want love, you have to *become* love.

This isn't fake positivity. It's not about pretending to be "high vibe" all the time. It's about choosing alignment. It's about noticing when your energy is off—and making the conscious choice to come back to center. To breathe. To ground. To lead from the inside out. The most powerful men don't chase energy—they *generate* it. They protect it. They know their vibe is their responsibility.

So ask yourself:

What am I emitting today?

What signal am I sending through my presence, my thoughts, my posture, my choices?

Because the energy you put out is the energy that comes back. You are not a victim of the world—you're a co-creator. And your frequency is your signature. Tune it with intention. Live it with integrity. Watch the world rise to meet you.

Synchronicities and Serendipity

When you start living in alignment—when your thoughts, actions, and energy are all moving in the same direction—something powerful begins to happen: life starts talking back to you.

You'll notice it in small ways at first. A conversation you needed to hear shows up at the exact right moment. A person you were just thinking about texts you. An opportunity appears out of nowhere, as if the universe was waiting for you to be ready.

These aren't just coincidences. They're *synchronicities*—winks from the universe that you're on the right path. Synchronicity is what happens when your inner world and the outer world begin to dance. It's life responding to your energy. And the more you trust yourself, the more you tune into your truth, the more frequently these moments appear.

Serendipity is the cousin of synchronicity. It's the unexpected magic. The blessings that seem to drop out of nowhere, even though deep down, you know they were always meant for you. These moments aren't forced. You don't chase them. They arrive when you're in flow—when you're open, aware, and fully present.

But here's the secret: you don't *create* synchronicity by trying to control life. You *allow* it by getting out of your own way. By staying in integrity. By keeping your frequency clean. By following your gut, even when logic can't explain why.

The Retained Man—the high-vibe man—starts to notice these moments more often. Because he's paying attention. He's listening. And because his energy is aligned, life begins to align with him. Call it divine timing. Call it intuition. Call it the universe, God, Source—whatever speaks to you.

The point is: when you're tuned in, life stops feeling random. It starts feeling *guided.*. So if things start clicking, doors start opening, or the right people suddenly appear—don't brush it off. Pay attention. Say thank you. Follow the breadcrumbs. Because synchronicity is not luck. It's a sign that you've entered the flow. And once you're in it, everything changes.

Deep Inner Peace and Mental Clarity

In a world that constantly pulls at your attention—notifications, noise, pressure to be *more*—peace becomes a radical act. Mental clarity becomes a superpower.

Most people are living in reaction mode. Always responding. Always chasing. Their minds are cluttered, their thoughts are loud, and even when things are going well, they don't feel calm. That's not living—that's surviving.

But deep inner peace? That's something different. That's power in stillness. It's not about escaping life—it's about being fully present *in* it, without being overwhelmed by it. It's the ability to sit with yourself and not feel restless. To move through the world without carrying its chaos inside of you. Peace doesn't mean nothing is happening. It means *you're not shaken by it.*

Clarity follows peace. When your mind is calm, you see truth more clearly. You stop reacting out of fear or urgency, and start responding from wisdom and intention. The fog lifts. Your next step becomes obvious. You stop second-guessing yourself because you *know* what's right.

But here's the key: you have to *protect* your peace. It's not handed to you—you create it. You earn it through boundaries, stillness, and self-awareness. You earn it by unplugging from the noise and plugging into what's real—your breath, your body, your inner knowing.

The high-vibe man doesn't let the outside world dictate his inner world. He's centered. Grounded. Clear. He speaks less, but when he does, it *lands*. He moves slower, but with more purpose. He's not running from anything. He's anchored in everything.

Peace and clarity don't come from controlling everything around you. They come from mastering what's *within* you. Still mind. Clear vision. Quiet strength. That's the mark of a man who's truly free. And once you've tasted that kind of peace, you'll never settle for noise again.

Meditation, Prayer & Higher Self Awareness

There's a deeper part of you that already knows the answers. It's not the voice that panics. It's not the one that doubts, compares, or overthinks. It's the calm, steady presence underneath it all—the part of you connected to something greater.

Tuning into that part is where real power begins.

Meditation and prayer aren't about escaping reality. They're about *connecting*— to yourself, to Source, to the higher wisdom that lives within and beyond you. These practices aren't about perfection or performance. They're about presence. They're about creating space in a world that never stops moving.

When you meditate, you quiet the noise so you can hear the truth. When you pray, you open your heart to guidance, trust, and surrender. When you do both, you begin to feel your *Higher Self*—the version of you that sees the bigger picture, that isn't ruled by fear, impulse, or ego.

The world trains men to stay in their heads. To think, analyze, grind. But your deepest wisdom doesn't come from your mind—it comes from your *alignment*. From that still, sacred space where your soul speaks. And you can only hear it when you slow down long enough to *listen*.

You don't have to sit on a mountaintop or chant in a cave. Meditation can be as simple as closing your eyes and breathing. Prayer can be a quiet conversation with the Divine, in your own words. It's not about ritual—it's about *relationship*.

The more you connect with your Higher Self, the more everything changes. You start making decisions from intuition, not anxiety. You become less reactive, more intentional. You feel guided—not just by logic, but by something deeper and wiser. This isn't about becoming someone else. It's about *returning* to who you've always been beneath the noise.

Start small. Sit in silence. Speak with honesty. Listen with an open heart. Your Higher Self is not far away. It's waiting for you—in the space between your thoughts, in the breath you forgot to take, in the stillness you've been avoiding. And once you meet Him, you'll never walk alone again.

Living With Intention, Not Impulse

A man ruled by impulse is like a ship without a compass—he moves, but he doesn't *know* where he's going. He reacts. He reaches. He grabs whatever's in front of him just to feel something. Food. Sex. Distraction. Approval. Quick hits of pleasure that never last.

But a man living with *intention*? That's a different energy entirely.

Intentional living is about choosing your direction—*before* the world chooses it for you. It's about waking up with purpose, not just waking up. It's about knowing what you stand for and making decisions that reflect it. Even when no one's watching. Especially then.

Impulse is fast. Impulse is loud. It wants comfort *now*. Intention is quiet. It's steady. It asks, *What does my highest self need—not just in this moment, but in the long run?*

When you live with intention, you stop leaking energy. You stop handing your power over to habits that numb you or people who drain you. You don't need to be perfect, but you become *aware*. You pause before reacting. You question before committing. You check in before checking out.

This isn't about control—it's about *consciousness*. It's about not letting your lower urges drive your life while your higher calling sits in the backseat. Living with intention means saying *no* to what pulls you away from your path, and *yes* to what deepens your alignment—even if it's uncomfortable. Even if it requires patience, discipline, or silence.

That's where true freedom lives. Not in doing whatever you want, whenever you feel like it—but in doing what *matters*, even when it's hard. So pause today. Ask yourself, *Am I moving with purpose? Or just reacting to whatever shows up?*

The impulsive man spends his life chasing fire. The intentional man *becomes* the flame. Live on purpose. Every moment. Every breath. That's the path to peace, power, and presence.

8

The New You

You're Not Just "Retaining" – You're Becoming

It's easy to think of retention as merely *not doing something*—as if it's all about avoidance, about holding back, about abstaining. But that view misses the point entirely. You're not just "retaining." You're **becoming**.

Every time you choose to honor your energy rather than leak it, you're sculpting a stronger version of yourself. You're not just holding onto your life force—you're building something with it. You're redirecting it, recycling it, refining it. That energy doesn't sit idle. It sharpens your mind. It deepens your presence. It fuels your evolution.

This is the shift: from restraint to refinement. From withholding to becoming whole. What you're doing isn't about denial—it's about design. You are designing the new you. One breath, one choice, one intention at a time. In a world that trains us to chase temporary highs, instant validation, and fleeting stimulation, *you* are choosing to anchor yourself in something deeper. You're choosing to be *rooted*, not restless.

So let go of the old narrative that you're "missing out" or "giving something up." You're not. You're tuning in. You're awakening to the richness of your inner landscape. You're learning how to channel that electric pulse within you—not just into productivity, but into purpose.

You're not just retaining. You're returning—to your power, to your presence, to your path. And most of all, you're becoming the person you were always meant to be.

Embodying the Warrior, the King, the Creator

To harness the life force within you is to remember who you truly are — not just as a human being navigating the world, but as a vessel of archetypal power. These ancient forces — the Warrior, the King, and the Creator — are not just metaphors. They are energies within your psyche, waiting to be awakened, integrated, and embodied.

The Warrior: Aligned Action and Unshakable Presence

The Warrior is not about aggression — it is about *clarity in motion*. The true Warrior doesn't fight for ego or control, but for alignment. This is the part of you that knows how to set boundaries, say "no" with strength, and stand firm in the face of fear. The Warrior moves forward despite resistance, not because they are without doubt, but because they are anchored in purpose.

To embody the Warrior:

- Identify your non-negotiables. What are you truly willing to stand for?

- Practice sacred discipline. Choose one habit each day that strengthens your focus and follow-through.

- Breathe into discomfort. The Warrior grows not by avoiding challenge, but by dancing with it consciously.

When your inner Warrior is active, you stop hesitating. You start creating momentum. You reclaim the energy that leaks through procrastination, people-pleasing, and avoidance.

The King: Sovereignty, Vision, and Inner Order

The King does not rule through domination. He governs through *presence*. The true King holds the center — the axis mundi — and from this still point, radiates stability and vision. When you activate your inner King, you are no longer thrown off by chaos. You become the eye of the storm.

To embody the King:

- Cultivate inner stillness. Meditation, solitude, or time in nature helps you connect with your center.

- Take full responsibility. The King doesn't blame or deflect. He owns his choices and their impact.

- Create sacred structure. The King builds kingdoms — whether in relationships, business, or inner world. He understands that chaos without direction leads to decay.

With the King alive in you, your confidence deepens. You feel your worth without needing to prove it. You lead not with force, but with gravitational strength.

The Creator: Flow, Imagination, and Sacred Expression

The Creator is the spark that turns vision into form. It is your innate ability to birth something from nothing — not just art, but solutions, innovations, ways of being. The Creator sees possibility in the unseen and has the courage to bring it into the light.

To embody the Creator:

- Make time to play. Creativity isn't always serious — it's wild, fluid, and unpredictable.

- Trust your intuition. The Creator doesn't follow maps. It follows inner knowing.

- Honor your unique voice. There is something that only *you* can say, do, or build. That is your sacred offering.

When you live from your Creator energy, life becomes art. Every challenge is a canvas. Every moment is an invitation to express the seed of life force that pulses within you.

Integration: The Sacred Trinity of Embodiment

These archetypes are not separate. They are facets of a whole. The Warrior gives you energy and movement. The King gives you structure and direction. The Creator gives you inspiration and uniqueness. Together, they create harmony — not perfection, but alignment.

When you embody the Warrior, the King, and the Creator, you stop reacting to life. You begin *shaping* it. From this place, your energy rises. Your confidence roots. Your clarity sharpens. And your seed within you begins to bloom.

Navigating the Modern World with Ancient Power

In a world of endless noise, notifications, and performance pressure, it's easy to feel untethered — as if your energy is constantly scattered, your clarity dulled, your power dimmed.

But beneath the surface of the modern grind lives something older, something wiser — a current that has never left you. This is the ancient power of life force: primal, intelligent, rooted. It is the seed within you that remembers. The modern world tells you to chase. Ancient power teaches you to *return*.

The Pace of Presence

Modern culture worships speed — but ancient power moves in rhythm. It listens. It waits. It *knows* when to strike, and when to still. To navigate this world with ancient power means learning how to slow down internally, even if everything around you is moving fast.

This is the art of presence. You become more effective not by doing more, but by being fully *in* what you're doing. One breath, one decision, one aligned action at a time.

"The wise one is not the busiest in the room, but the most rooted."

Discernment Over Distraction

Technology is not the enemy. But unconscious use of it is. Every scroll, every ping, every dopamine hit can siphon away your power — unless you learn to choose consciously. Ancient power gives you *discernment*. It reminds you that your attention is sacred. Where you place it shapes your reality.

To reclaim your focus:

- Start your day without screens. Begin with breath, stillness, or intention.

- Ask yourself throughout the day: "Is this feeding my life force or draining it?"

- Protect your inner world like a sacred temple. Not everything and everyone gets access.

Stillness in the Storm

Life today is loud. But power is quiet. True strength isn't reactive. It doesn't need to prove itself. It *listens deeply*. Ancient power is the ability to hold chaos without becoming it. You don't have to match the energy of the world around you. You can rise above it — not with ego, but with essence.

"You are not here to survive the world. You are here to *shape* it."

Ancient power gives you the grounded confidence to lead without shouting, to love without grasping, and to live without betraying your soul's truth.

The Modern Mystic: A Bridge Between Worlds

You are not here to escape the world. You are here to bring the ancient into the now — to become a living bridge between wisdom and action, between soul and structure. This is the path of the modern mystic, the embodied leader, the awake creator.

To walk this path is to remember:

- Your breath is technology.

- Your body is intelligence.

- Your intuition is data.

- Your stillness is a weapon.

When you navigate the modern world with ancient power, you stop outsourcing your authority. You become the source. Your energy stabilizes. Your confidence becomes embodied. And your clarity cuts through the noise like a blade of light.

Long-Term Retention: Myths, Cycles & Balance

When we speak of "retention," we are not simply talking about holding back. We are talking about *holding power*. About choosing presence over impulse. Intention over reaction. Vision over momentary release.

Whether in the realm of sexual energy, creative flow, or inner discipline, long-term retention is often misunderstood. It's not about repression or control. It's about *cultivation* — learning to direct your energy with wisdom and purpose.

Myth #1: Retention Equals Suppression

One of the biggest misconceptions about long-term retention is that it means cutting yourself off from pleasure, desire, or expression. This is not true retention — it's resistance. And resistance always creates tension, imbalance, and eventually burnout.

True retention is *integration*. It's the conscious choice to hold energy in a way that nourishes you. To feel desire fully, and not be ruled by it. To ride the waves without being thrown by them.

"It's not about shutting the door. It's about learning when to open it, and why."

116

Myth #2: More Days = More Power

While discipline is powerful, numbers alone don't tell the whole story. Retention is not a scoreboard — it's a relationship. The quality of your awareness matters more than the quantity of your streak. Without grounding, you can become inflated. Without flow, stagnation sets in. Retention must serve *balance*, not ego.

You're not here to hoard energy. You're here to *circulate* it. To turn stored life force into clarity, presence, vision, and creation.

Cycles: The Body's Natural Rhythm

Energy moves in cycles. So do you. There are seasons for building, and seasons for releasing. Times when retention feels powerful, and times when letting go becomes the medicine. The key is not to cling to one state, but to listen. To trust the intelligence of your body, your nervous system, your soul.

Ask yourself regularly:

- Am I retaining out of fear, or out of intention?

- Is my energy rising, or becoming stagnant?

- What am I doing with the energy I'm holding?

When you learn to *cooperate* with your cycles rather than override them, you stay in balance. You remain both rooted and rising.

Balance: Channelling, Not Containing

Long-term retention is only powerful when it becomes *creative*. If you're holding back but not transmuting, the energy can turn on you — manifesting as frustration, anxiety, or restlessness.

But when you channel that same energy — into movement, writing, vision, connection, or service — it becomes magnetic. Alchemical. Alive.

117

"Retention without redirection is just storage. But when you channel what you hold, you become a conduit for life itself."

Balance is the middle path. It's where sacred discipline meets embodied freedom. It's knowing when to hold and when to release. When to pause and when to act. It's living as an artist with your own energy.

Remember This

You don't retain energy to escape the world. You retain to meet it more fully — with clarity, with confidence, with calm intensity. Long-term retention is not about being perfect. It's about being *present*. About listening. Honoring your energy not as a resource to be spent, but as a force to be *shaped*. Balance isn't a destination. It's a dance. And you are the dancer, the rhythm, and the drum.

Building a Life Worth Retaining For

Retention is only meaningful if there is something *worth holding your power for*. It's not about willpower for the sake of discipline. It's about devotion. Purpose. Vision. A life designed with such clarity and soul that it becomes an *honor* to hold your energy — because you *know* what you're building with it.

You weren't born just to survive, to grind, to repeat. You're here to create something real — a life that feels sacred from the inside out.

What Are You Building?

This is the deeper invitation: not just to retain energy, but to *aim* it. To move from drifting into designing. From reacting to *responding* — with purpose.

Ask yourself:

- What kind of man or woman am I becoming?

- What legacy am I shaping, through my energy, choices, and presence?

- What would my life look like if I lived with full integrity to my deepest values?

When you can answer that — even imperfectly — everything shifts. Retention becomes natural. Clarity replaces chaos. Vision replaces temptation. You stop running from short-term gratification because you're too devoted to long-term creation.

Make Your Life Magnetic

A life worth retaining for doesn't mean a perfect one. It means a life that feels *aligned*. It means creating environments, habits, relationships, and goals that call your highest self forward. A life where the inner world and the outer world are no longer at war — but working in harmony.

Build a life where:

- Your mornings anchor you.

- Your work lights you up or stretches you toward growth.

- Your relationships reflect depth, not just distraction.

- Your time is a container for creativity, not consumption.

- Your energy is directed toward something bigger than ego — something sacred.

"The more meaningful your life becomes, the easier it is to hold your power. Because now, you *know* where it's going."

Purpose Makes Retention Effortless

You don't have to fight urges when you're filled with purpose. You don't need to force discipline when your life calls your greatness forward every single day.

That's the secret: make your life so aligned, so compelling, that you *want* to show up fully. That you can't afford to leak energy anymore — because the vision you're carrying is too important to delay.

119

Let your life be the reason you rise early. The reason you stay focused. The reason you breathe deeper, move stronger, love more honestly. You retain, because you are building. You hold, because what you're holding *for* is worth everything.

Remember This

You're not here to just practice retention. You're here to *live retention*. To create, to love, to lead with the full force of who you are. Make your life worthy of your energy. And your energy will serve your life.

9

The Mission

From Self-Help to Selfless Purpose

There comes a point on every inner journey when the focus naturally shifts—from personal growth to greater impact. What begins as a quest to feel better, to heal, to become more energized or confident, subtly transforms into something deeper: a calling to serve, uplift, and contribute. This shift marks the movement from self-help to selfless purpose.

At the beginning, self-help is necessary. It's the oxygen mask on the plane—you can't support anyone else if you're suffocating. We read the books, do the breathwork, journal through the pain, and gradually reclaim our power. These practices aren't selfish; they are foundational. They awaken the seed within us—the dormant vitality, clarity, and courage waiting to sprout.

But once that seed begins to grow, it naturally seeks expression beyond the self. Confidence becomes conviction. Energy turns into momentum. Clarity reveals direction. And that direction often points toward others—toward service, toward contribution, toward being a vessel for something greater than personal success.

This is not about abandoning yourself. It's about realizing that the more deeply you know and nurture your inner life, the more powerfully you can show up for the world around you. You stop chasing goals just to feel worthy, and start living with a mission that *makes* life feel worthy.

Your self-help journey becomes the soil from which selfless purpose blooms. And in that purpose, you don't lose yourself—you find a deeper version of yourself. One who is connected, committed, and capable of making a meaningful difference. So as you cultivate the seed within, ask not only "How can I grow?" but also, "Where can I give?" The answer to that question may just be your mission in disguise.

Becoming a Lighthouse in a Dark World

In times of confusion, crisis, or collective uncertainty, it's easy to feel small. What can one person do in the face of so much noise, pain, and complexity? The answer is both humbling and profound: you can become a lighthouse. A lighthouse doesn't chase ships. It doesn't scream directions. It simply stands in its stillness—anchored, lit, and clear. And in doing so, it guides. It protects. It saves.

Becoming a lighthouse is not about having all the answers. It's not about fixing the world or forcing change. It's about embodying clarity in the midst of chaos, becoming a steady source of presence and perspective for those still lost in the storm. Your energy becomes your message. Your life becomes the light.

This kind of leadership doesn't require a title or a platform. It begins in the everyday—in how you speak to yourself, how you show up for others, how you hold your values when no one is watching. When you commit to living from your inner light, you radiate a quiet power that others can feel. You give them permission to reconnect with their own.

The world doesn't need more noise. It needs more signals. It needs more people who are willing to do the inner work, rise with grace, and hold space for others without trying to control them. That's the true mission—not to be impressive, but to be *illuminating*.

And the beautiful thing about light is this: you don't have to force it. You just have to uncover what's already inside you. Tend to your seed, fuel your flame, and trust that even the smallest glow can change the course of someone else's journey. You were never meant to blend into the fog. You were meant to be seen—from the shore, from the sea, from the soul.

Teaching Without Preaching

There's a fine line between guiding and dictating, between sharing wisdom and forcing it. True teaching—transformative teaching—doesn't come from superiority. It comes from embodiment.

When your life reflects the truth you've discovered, you don't need to preach. People feel it. They sense the alignment between your words and your presence, and that quiet coherence becomes the most powerful lesson of all.

To teach without preaching is to trust that others are on their own sacred timeline. It's understanding that awakening can't be rushed or imposed—it must be *remembered*, and often remembered through experience, not instruction. Your role isn't to wake people up by shaking them; it's to stand awake yourself, and invite them to do the same when they're ready.

This approach is grounded in humility. It recognizes that we're all still learning, no matter how far we've come. And so we teach not from a mountaintop, but from the middle of the path. We speak from wounds that have been tended, not hidden. We offer tools, not rules. We share our stories, not sermons.

The mission, then, is not to convert anyone to your way, but to live your way so fully that it naturally inspires others to discover their own. You plant seeds through kindness, curiosity, and calm consistency—not pressure. You become the mirror in which others can see their own potential more clearly. And in this way, you teach the most important lesson of all: that wisdom lives within them, too.

Legacy, Fatherhood & Brotherhood

At some point, the mission becomes less about what you *achieve* and more about what you *leave behind*. Legacy isn't carved in trophies or titles—it's etched into lives touched, hearts guided, and values passed forward.

For many, this awareness awakens most deeply through fatherhood—not only biological, but spiritual and emotional as well. To be a father is to become a living bridge between what came before and what will come after. It's a sacred responsibility: not to control the path of another, but to clear the way, to model integrity, to protect what matters, and to embody the strength that nurtures, not dominates.

Fatherhood calls us into a higher version of ourselves—not perfect, but present. The kind of presence that says, "I'm here. I may not have all the answers, but I will stand beside you, guide you, and walk with you while you discover your own."

And then there's brotherhood—the forgotten medicine of the modern man. In a world that often teaches men to compete, isolate, or suppress, brotherhood invites us back to connection. It says: You don't have to carry this alone. You're not the only one figuring it out. We rise, not by proving ourselves, but by holding each other accountable to our truth—with compassion, with honesty, and with fire when needed.

Legacy is not an end point. It's being lived right now—in how you show up for your child, your partner, your brothers, your community. It's the echo of your presence long after you're gone. Every word you speak, every hand you extend, every moment you choose love over fear—you are shaping it.

So ask yourself not just, *What will I build?* but *Who will I become in the building?* Not just *What will I leave behind?* but *Who will carry it forward because of how I loved, how I led, and how I lived?* This is the mission. To be the man your younger self needed, and the man your future lineage will thank.

The Retained Man's Code

In a world that rewards instant gratification, the retained man walks a different path. He is not driven by urge, but by intention. Not swayed by chaos, but anchored in clarity. He doesn't waste his life force chasing fleeting highs—he *harnesses* it, holds it, refines it.

Retention, in its truest sense, isn't just about holding back—it's about *holding power*. It's about choosing mastery over indulgence, purpose over pleasure, vision over distraction. The retained man guards his energy like sacred currency, knowing every choice he makes either invests in his mission—or steals from it.

His code is simple, but not easy. It requires discipline, integrity, and devotion to something greater than comfort. It's a quiet strength. A deep-rooted fire. A presence that speaks louder than performance.

The Retained Man's Code:

- **I do not chase—I attract through alignment.**

  I become what I seek. I magnetize through embodiment, not pursuit.

- **I do not waste—I invest.**

  My energy is sacred. My attention is valuable. I choose where it flows.

- **I speak less, move more.**

  My actions reflect my values. My presence is my message.

- **I don't suppress—I transmute.**

  Desire becomes drive. Pain becomes purpose. Instinct becomes intention.

- **I remain grounded, even when tested.**

  The storm does not define me. My roots go deeper than the noise.

- **I honor the feminine without becoming dependent on it.**
  I meet her in strength, not in need. I see her, but I do not lose myself in her.

- **I lead myself first.**

  I take full ownership of my path, my choices, my mission.

This code is not a performance—it's a practice. It's not about becoming perfect, but becoming *whole*. Each day is a chance to sharpen the sword, to walk with more purpose, to hold more light. Because a retained man is not just retaining seed—he's retaining vision, clarity, energy, and truth. And from that reservoir, he leads.

Conclusion

You Are the Seed

As we reach the end of this journey together, remember this: you are not merely someone seeking purpose, energy, or clarity. You are the seed. Every aspect of your life, your potential, your mission—everything begins with the simple yet profound truth that the seed exists within you, waiting to sprout, grow, and transform into something extraordinary.

You are the embodiment of possibility. Within you is the energy to change, the strength to overcome, and the wisdom to lead. But just as a seed requires nourishment, patience, and the right environment to grow, so too does your potential. You must cultivate the soil, water it with intention, and shield it from the elements that threaten to block its rise.

The seed isn't just a metaphor—it's the core of who you are. It's your energy, your soul's purpose, your deepest calling. And as you continue to nurture and protect it, it will become something powerful. It will become your legacy, your impact, your mission. It will bloom into the life you've always imagined—and more, because the seed contains far more than you can yet comprehend.

Know this: the seed doesn't question its worth. It doesn't wonder if it's enough. It simply trusts in its process, in its time. In the same way, trust in your unfolding. Trust that you are enough. Trust that everything you need is already within you. You are not waiting for permission. You are not waiting for a perfect moment. You are the seed, already planted. And with every choice you make to live with intention, to move with confidence, and to embrace clarity, you are nurturing the conditions necessary for your growth.

You are the seed. And what you become is limitless.

Your Journey Continues

As this chapter closes, know that your journey is far from over—it's just beginning. The seed you've planted within you has already begun to sprout. You've nurtured it with awareness, with discipline, with vision. But the growth doesn't stop here. This book, these words, the practices, and the insights shared—they are not a destination. They are a map. They are tools. They are the compass pointing toward the unfolding of your greater purpose.

Every day you walk this path, you are called to deepen your connection with your own life force. You will face challenges, setbacks, moments of doubt—and in those moments, you'll find the strength to recommit. Because the journey is not linear. Growth doesn't come in a straight line. It's cyclical. It's full of ebbs and flows, of expanding and contracting. But each step, each decision, each moment you choose to honor your seed, you move closer to the person you are meant to become.

You will find that as you continue, you have more energy than you once thought possible. Confidence will become second nature. Clarity will become your guide. And soon, the life you envision won't just be a dream—it will be your reality.

Remember that the mission you've chosen is not a burden; it's a blessing. The seed within you is a gift, and as it grows, it brings not only clarity and purpose to your life but also to those around you. Your growth will ripple out into your relationships, your work, your community. As you expand, so does your impact.

So, as you turn the page and step forward into the next chapter of your life, don't think of this as the end of the journey. Think of it as the moment you embark on the greatest adventure: the ongoing journey of becoming. The mission doesn't stop. It only deepens. And you, the seed, are destined to grow into something magnificent.

Your journey continues. And it is full of endless possibility.

Final Words of Encouragement

As you close this book and reflect on the words within these pages, remember that you are not alone on this path. The journey you're on is one that countless others have walked before you, and countless others will walk after you. But there is something unique about your journey—something powerful, something only you can bring into the world.

There will be times when the road feels uncertain, when you question your choices, or when doubt creeps in. And that's okay. Doubt is a natural part of growth. It's a sign that you're pushing beyond your comfort zone, stretching into new realms of possibility. The seed doesn't question whether it will grow—it simply trusts the process. And so, too, can you trust your own growth, even in moments of uncertainty.

Trust that the energy you invest into yourself, into your mission, and into your life force will always return to you, multiplied. Trust that the clarity you seek will come—not in an instant, but over time, through practice, reflection, and faith. Confidence isn't something you have all at once—it's a muscle that grows stronger the more you use it.

The challenges ahead are not roadblocks; they are opportunities to deepen your connection to your truth, to build resilience, and to sharpen your focus. Every moment, every decision, every action you take is another opportunity to live more fully in alignment with the seed within you.

So be kind to yourself. Celebrate each step, no matter how small. Know that every seed needs time, patience, and care to fully blossom. But with persistence, with presence, and with faith in the process, you will emerge as the person you are meant to be.

The world is waiting for you—not the version of you that you *think* you should be, but the truest, most authentic version of you. The one who understands that your energy is sacred, your clarity is your compass, and your confidence is a gift to the world.

You've already planted the seed. Now, trust that it will grow.

Appendices

90-Day Retention Journal Template

Introduction to Your 90-Day Journey

Before you begin, take a moment to reflect on your current state and what you hope to achieve in the next 90 days. This journal is designed to support your journey of growth, retention, and mastery. Each day, you'll be asked to reflect on key areas that will help you stay aligned with your energy, purpose, and clarity.

Daily Journal Template

Date: _____

Focus for Today: (What is your primary focus today in terms of energy, clarity, or confidence?)

- What is the key task or intention for today?

- What challenge or distraction do you want to stay focused through?

Morning Reflection:

(Connect with your inner energy before starting your day)

- How do I feel in my body this morning?

- What is one thing I can do today to retain my energy and keep my focus?

_____

_____

Evening Reflection:

(Reflect on the day's progress, how you've retained or redirected your energy)

- How did I honor my energy today? What choices did I make that aligned with my mission?

_____

_____

- Did I face any distractions or challenges? How did I respond to them?

_____

_____

- What is one thing I learned today about myself and my journey?

_____

_____

Weekly Check-In

Every week, take a step back and evaluate your overall progress. Use this space to reflect on the trends you've noticed and celebrate your growth.

Week: _____

What were my major wins this week?

(Identify the moments where you stayed aligned with your purpose and energy)

_____

_____

What challenges did I face, and how did I grow through them?

_____

_____

What have I learned about my retention and life force this week?

_____

_____

How can I refine my focus for the coming week?

_____

_____

_____

Midpoint Reflection (Day 45)

At the halfway mark, reflect deeply on your journey so far. This is an opportunity to recalibrate and make adjustments if needed.

How has my energy been this far? Have I retained or leaked it?

_____

_____

Am I aligned with my mission and purpose?

_____

_____

What is one area of my life where I feel more clarity and confidence?

_____

_____

What area needs further attention or refinement?

_____

_____

_____

End of 90 Days Reflection

After completing 90 days, take a moment to look back at your journey. What changes have you noticed? How has your energy, confidence, and clarity shifted?

How have I grown over these 90 days?

_____

_____

What were my key lessons learned during this time?

_____

_____

What new habits or practices will I continue going forward?

_____

_____

How will I keep nurturing the seed within me?

_____

_____

What is my next step in this ongoing journey?

_____

_____

_____

Reflection Prompts for the Journey:

1. **Energy Retention:**

   o   What areas of your life tend to drain your energy? How can you begin to create boundaries or practices to protect your energy?

2. **Confidence:**

   o   When you feel confident, what does it look like? What are you doing differently? How can you start practicing that confidence every day?

3. **Clarity:**

   o   How do you tap into clarity in moments of uncertainty? What practices, such as meditation or journaling, help you find your center?

4. **Legacy:**

   o   As you continue to grow, what impact do you want to leave behind? How are you aligning with your greater mission every day?

This journal is a tool for deepening your connection to your life force and purpose. By staying consistent, taking time to reflect, and adjusting as you go, you'll be nurturing the seed within you and cultivating the life you desire.

Recommended Resources (Books, Videos, Apps)

Recommended Books

1. **The Power of Now** by Eckhart Tolle

   A powerful guide to living in the present moment and cultivating inner peace and clarity.

2. **Atomic Habits** by James Clear

   Learn how small habits compound to create massive change, with practical advice on habit formation and retention of energy.

3. **The Four Agreements** by Don Miguel Ruiz

   A guide to personal freedom through four simple but profound agreements that can change your life.

4. **The Untethered Soul** by Michael A. Singer

   Explore how to release limiting thoughts and beliefs and connect to your deeper, true self.

5. **The Art of Power** by Thich Nhat Hanh

   A beautiful reflection on the intersection of mindfulness and leadership, helping you to harness your energy with wisdom and compassion.

6. **Man's Search for Meaning** by Viktor E. Frankl

   A life-changing perspective on finding purpose, even in the most difficult of circumstances.

7. **You Are a Badass** by Jen Sincero

   An empowering, no-nonsense approach to unlocking confidence and living your best life.

8. **The Wisdom of Insecurity** by Alan Watts

   Dive into the teachings of Alan Watts on letting go of the need for certainty and living in alignment with your energy and purpose.

9. **The Power of Intention** by Wayne Dyer

   This book helps you understand how to consciously connect with your life force and use it to manifest your desires.

10. **The Seven Spiritual Laws of Success** by Deepak Chopra

    A blend of practical advice and spiritual wisdom to guide you on your journey of success, alignment, and fulfilment.

Recommended Videos & Documentaries

1. **The Secret (2006)**

   A documentary exploring the Law of Attraction and how we can manifest the life we desire by focusing on our energy and intentions.

2. **Tony Robbins: I Am Not Your Guru (2016)**

   A behind-the-scenes look at Tony Robbins' life-changing seminars, focusing on personal growth and mastering energy for success.

3. **Inner Worlds, Outer Worlds (2012)**

   This documentary explores the connection between our inner energy and the world around us through ancient wisdom and modern science.

4. **Eckhart Tolle: The Power of Presence** (YouTube)

   Eckhart Tolle offers insights into living a life free from mental clutter and embracing the present moment.

5. **You Are What You Believe** by Dr. Joe Dispenza (YouTube)
   Dr. Joe Dispenza explores how your beliefs shape your reality and how to harness the power of your mind to heal and grow.

6. **Brené Brown: The Power of Vulnerability (TED Talk)**

   A transformative TED Talk by Brené Brown, teaching how embracing vulnerability can lead to greater connection and courage.

7. **The Mind Explained** (Netflix Series)

   This series breaks down different aspects of the human mind—memory, anxiety, mindfulness—helping you understand your mental landscape and how to harness your energy.

8. **I Am (2010)**

   A thought-provoking documentary that delves into questions of human connection, purpose, and the life force that binds us all.

Recommended Apps

1. **Headspace**
   A user-friendly meditation app that helps you develop mindfulness, clarity, and emotional balance through guided sessions.

2. **Calm**
   An app for relaxation, mindfulness, and sleep, offering guided meditation, breathing exercises, and soothing soundscapes.

3. **Insight Timer**

   A free meditation app with thousands of guided meditations, music tracks, and talks from spiritual leaders and teachers.

4. **MyFitnessPal**
   A health app that allows you to track your nutrition, fitness, and energy levels, helping you maintain physical well-being as part of your holistic growth.

5. **Forest: Stay Focused**

   A productivity app that helps you stay focused and retain your energy by encouraging you to put down your phone and concentrate on your work.

6. **Aura**
   A mindfulness app offering short meditations, sleep stories, and calming music to restore your mental and emotional energy.

7. **Gratitude Journal**

   An app for daily reflections and gratitude practice to help you stay centered, positive, and focused on the abundance around you.

8. **Breethe**
   A comprehensive app for meditation, sleep, breathing exercises, and mindfulness to help you balance your energy and emotions.

9. **Superhuman**
   A productivity app designed to help you organize your tasks in a way that supports energy and focus, aligning with your larger life mission.

10. **Daily Yoga**

An app for daily yoga sessions that help you build strength, balance, and awareness, supporting physical energy retention and clarity.

These resources will help you continue your journey of self-mastery, energy retention, and personal growth, supporting the mission you've already begun. Whether you're looking to dive deeper into spiritual teachings, cultivate mindfulness, or strengthen your physical vitality, these books, videos, and apps offer valuable tools to guide you along the way.

FAQs About Semen Retention

---

1. What is semen retention?

Answer: Semen retention is the practice of intentionally abstaining from ejaculation in order to preserve and redirect sexual energy. This energy is believed to enhance mental clarity, increase physical vitality, and promote spiritual growth.

2. What are the benefits of semen retention?

Answer: Advocates of semen retention claim it can lead to improved energy levels, heightened focus, increased confidence, better physical health, and a stronger connection to one's purpose. Some also report emotional balance and a greater sense of mental clarity and spiritual awareness.

3. How long should I practice semen retention?

Answer: The duration of practice varies from person to person. Some choose to practice for a few days, weeks, or even months. It's essential to listen to your body and only retain for as long as you feel aligned with the practice. Many people start with 30 days and build from there.

4. Is semen retention safe?

Answer: Yes, for most men, semen retention is generally considered safe when practiced mindfully. It's important to avoid the practice becoming a source of frustration or stress. As with any lifestyle change, it's wise to pay attention to your body and consult a healthcare professional if needed.

5. Can semen retention help with confidence and energy?

Answer: Many practitioners report higher levels of confidence, energy, and clarity as a result of semen retention. The idea is that by conserving sexual energy, it is redirected to other areas of life—such as physical health, creativity, and personal growth—leading to an increase in overall vitality and self-assurance.

6. What are the spiritual benefits of semen retention?

Answer: Spiritually, semen retention is seen as a way to cultivate and conserve life force energy (often referred to as "Qi" or "prana"). By holding onto this energy, practitioners believe they can raise their vibration, increase spiritual awareness, and deepen their connection to their higher purpose.

7. Does semen retention affect physical performance or health?

Answer: Some men report enhanced athletic performance, muscle recovery, and overall vitality after practicing semen retention. The theory is that by retaining semen, the body's energy is directed toward rejuvenation, physical strength, and muscle growth. However, the effects can vary based on individual health and lifestyle.

8. What are the challenges of practicing semen retention?

Answer: One of the primary challenges is dealing with sexual urges and maintaining discipline. It can be mentally and emotionally demanding, especially in the early stages. Additionally, some individuals may experience frustration or tension as they adjust to the practice. It's important to approach the practice with patience and self-compassion.

9. Can semen retention help with self-control and discipline?

Answer: Yes, many people find that semen retention strengthens their willpower and self-discipline. The practice requires a high level of control and mindfulness, which can translate to other areas of life—such as work, relationships, and personal development.

10. Will I experience physical discomfort during semen retention?

Answer: Some men may experience discomfort or sexual frustration when they first start practicing semen retention. This is a natural part of the process, as the body adjusts. Over time, many find that the urges become easier to manage. However, if physical discomfort persists, it's important to assess your approach and consult a medical professional if necessary.

11. Can I practice semen retention if I'm in a relationship?

Answer: Yes, semen retention can be practiced while in a relationship. Many couples find that it enhances intimacy and emotional connection. However, open communication is key, especially if both partners are not aligned with the practice. It's essential to navigate the practice with understanding, mutual respect, and healthy communication.

12. What is the difference between semen retention and celibacy?

Answer: Semen retention is focused specifically on withholding ejaculation while still engaging in sexual activity, whereas celibacy generally refers to abstaining from all forms of sexual activity. While both practices aim to conserve sexual energy, they differ in terms of scope and lifestyle choice.

13. How does semen retention affect mental clarity and focus?

Answer: Many practitioners report a significant boost in mental clarity and focus during periods of semen retention. The energy that would otherwise be expended is thought to be redirected to the mind, leading to increased concentration, clearer thinking, and enhanced cognitive function.

14. Should I practice semen retention if I'm experiencing sexual frustration?

Answer: If sexual frustration is intense, it may be helpful to explore other avenues of releasing pent-up energy, such as physical activity, meditation, or creative pursuits. Practicing semen retention should not create more stress or frustration. It's important to be patient and mindful of your emotional and physical needs.

15. Is there any scientific evidence supporting the benefits of semen retention?

Answer: While there is limited scientific research on the specific practice of semen retention, there are studies on related topics, such as the effects of sexual abstinence and energy conservation on mental and physical health. Many of the reported benefits come from anecdotal evidence and personal testimonies, but more research is needed to fully understand its effects.

16. Can semen retention improve my relationships?

Answer: Some practitioners believe that semen retention can improve relationships by deepening emotional intimacy, fostering better communication, and cultivating more mindful and loving sexual encounters. Retaining energy is thought to help partners connect on a deeper, more spiritual level.

17. How do I begin practicing semen retention?

Answer: To begin, set an intention for your practice. Start small—perhaps by committing to a short period of time, such as 7 or 14 days. Pay attention to your energy, emotions, and physical sensations. Use mindfulness and breathwork to manage urges, and approach the practice with patience and self-compassion.